angus

Also by Charles Siebert

• • •

WICKERBY
An Urban Pastoral

angus

A Memoir

CHARLES SIEBERT

Crown Publishers
New York

Published by Crown Publishers, New York, New York.
Member of the Crown Publishing Group.

Random House, Inc. New York, Toronto, London, Sydney, Auckland

www.randomhouse.com

CROWN is a trademark and the Crown colophon
is a registered trademark of Random House, Inc.

Printed in the United States of America

DESIGN BY LYNNE AMFT

Library of Congress Cataloging-in-Publication Data
Siebert, Charles.
  Angus : a memoir / Charles Siebert.
    1. Jack Russell terrier—Fiction. 2. Dogs—Fiction. I. Title.
PS3569.I357 A84 2000
813'.54—dc21
                                                    99-086318

ISBN 0-609-60494-5

10 9 8 7 6 5 4 3 2 1

First Edition

For Bex . . .
In memory of Angus

acknowledgments

My thanks to Muriel and Ronald Hallet, of Pollard's Combe, for their good nature and, of course, for the gift of Angus.

I'm very grateful to Ms. Maureen Sinclair for the use of her cottage in St. Just, Cornwall, where Angus was able to spend the first months of his life out along the ocean cliffs.

And to the Bedfords—Helen, Paul, Jack, and Tom—for the use of their London home in the weeks before Angus's departure to the States.

To the sisters Nostro, Beverly, and Gerri, thank you for taking such good care of our other dog, Lucy, when we couldn't be there for her.

ACKNOWLEDGMENTS

I'd like to thank my editor, Ann Patty, for offering just the right measure of encouragement and healthy skepticism to get me through this odd endeavor.

Warm thanks, as well, to Gerry Marzorati, Christopher Merrill, Lisa Chase, Susan Prospere, Jeffrey Greene, Francisco Goldman, Ben Anastas, Nicholas Dawidoff, Scott Anderson, Jon Lee Anderson, Manny Howard, Mark Freeman, Freda Garmaise, Mary Cybulski, John Tintori, Robert and Joseph Siebert, and Francis and Marion V. Siebert, for lending their ears and support, especially during the early, most uncertain stages.

Finally, I want to thank my agent, Chuck Verrill, who repeatedly goes out of his way to keep me going.

They [the Huron] believe that souls are immortal, and that when they leave the body they go at once to dance and rejoice . . . , taking the route and the way of stars, which they call Atiskein andahatey, *the path of souls, which we call the Milky Way. . . . They say that the souls of dogs go there also by way of certain stars which are near neighbors to the soul's path, and which they call* Gagnenon andahatey, *that is to say, the path of dogs.*

FATHER SAGARD-THEODAT,
The Long Journey to the Country of the Hurons
(1632)

1

IF I COULD LIFT MYSELF AND RUN AGAIN. If I could run here to the far wood's edge, where it has just happened, at night; run away from the very place I'll have to crawl back to now—and why? What is it, exactly, drawing me to those cabin lights?—lift myself and run here to the far wood's edge, directly beneath the bottom right corner star of the Big Dipper's ladle, where it all happened, I would.

"An—gus?" "An—gus?"

Cries. Theirs. Some deep. Some higher and thin. I heard them, not very long ago, but hazily, when it was already too late, when I had just awakened, I think, to find myself ruined like this, and numb, and the world so oddly pitched that I hadn't even begun to consider the long climb back out from among these trees through the side field under the Big Dipper toward the cabin lights where they, my owners, sit tonight.

It was already too late, and I so small and low, lying here among the trees behind the field of uncut grass, that they couldn't see me. Not the way they each came outside and looked, so tentative, into darkness, calling toward the woods, calling out across the night in my general direction but still standing so firmly behind whatever boundary it is that you have, and that never existed for me: darkness and the woods and their mind-mate, fear.

Can you stand, can you even imagine it anymore? Did you ever know it at all: full-fathom fearlessness and the feel of charging away from your own lit windows into the night, charging off on a scent, purely, and the urge that it stirs. Go. Go. And further, and on, with nothing holding you back, no worry, not a second, not even a first, thought—thought that leads to fear and fear to worries and these to clouded thoughts, like the fence-snagged sheep hair of atmosphere that drags tonight in a blue wind about the planet.

Peepers. I hear the peepers down at the back pond and crickets. I hear the maddening, mounting measures of mosquito drone mercifully erased now by the swooping bats. So many stars out, swimming, flowing, endlessly, through the Dipper's bottomless cup. Atoms, everywhere. I see, but I can't stop them. I'm coming apart. I'm little more now than the sum of those peepers, sounding.

2

HOW DID I COME TO THIS? I've never been one to look back. I've never known regret. That's your province, isn't it, the mind-mate of expectation? Something I'm not saddled with beyond the immediate kind: you go out the door. I hunker down and wait, mangling some prized possession of yours to ease my loneliness.

You sit around all day and stare off blankly through windows. I wait for you to finally get past your brains' alien entanglements and take me out for a walk.

You hover interminably above kitchen counters, blabbing, on and on, while I wait for you to finally put down the food bowl.

But as for long-term imaginings, the ability to get worked up over a possible future that doesn't at all resemble any one day: an endless series of filled food bowls, and of the best walks I've ever known, and ongoing nights in which you never leave me—hope, in other words, I wasn't even aware such a thing existed until now. Until, lying here at the edge of my own absence, I'm suddenly able to imagine in their faces the look of the hopes I've dashed.

I can't say how it happened. All I remember is a scent, rising, above all others, growing stronger as I ran toward it and then hard and sharp: a scissor-flash of fangs and my body going with the stars and the distant cabin lights into a swirl that, all at once, stopped with me, hard, against the earth, and the scent falling away, fading, far back into the forest.

"An—gus?"

Cries. Theirs.

Are they what stirred, what arrested me a while ago when I was slipping away? Are they what's keeping me here now, still snagged and adrift within the sphere of worry, when I was already well on my way, frictionless, around the next bend? And hasn't that always been the complaint about me, that I'm forever straining at the lead, trying to see what lies in store, just up ahead?

It's late. I'm cold. Peepers. Those pond peepers sounding, still, in the dark woods behind me, like mud-embedded stars, each peep a deep burst of light, one connecting to the next, and somehow, in their chorus, comprising my consciousness.

I'm beginning to see everything now, but backward, in recollection, as though my last flash forward into this forest is illuminating a final flashback: the things that I wasn't thinking when I charged out tonight; the steady train of events, from my life's very beginning, that lead, inevitably, here, to these dark woods, and the scissor fangs, and those far-off cabin lights where they sit now, in the warmth, leaning, I'm certain, for some indication of me.

3

ANGUS. THEY CALL ME ANGUS. I go by and, when it suits me, come to, Angus. That's the name I was given one day nine months ago, the day that they suddenly appeared at Pollard's Combe and set off the chain of events that would eventually thrust me here, where I now lie at the dark edge of a new-world forest.

The thrust of chance. That's everything, isn't it, from the very beginning? One day, like one of those sudden rain squalls that were always sweeping in off the seas of my native England, you arrive, sideways, into atmosphere, a pair of eyes and attendant senses, receiving.

And the only questions are: Is it a covered, a framed part of a day that you've entered, or an open and a roofless one? Is there a bed, of any kind, or is it the hard ground of some disowned plot, a back alley somewhere within the streets and spires of cemented smells that you call a city?

Or the ground, perhaps, of a place far enough away from you and all of your buildings that at least there isn't the added burden of human pity to bear, and a creature can just crawl off and make its own way the best that it can.

Me, I got a bit of straw in the corner of a stone barn on a September morning eleven months ago, the barn of an old Devon cow farm situated at the far end of a long narrow lane that winds its way up out of the seaside village of Slapton. The road courses inland through miles of high tufted hedgerows that lead, eventually, down a steep grade to two stone pillars with a little sign in the grass before them: Pollard's Combe.

I can still see, still smell it—the sweet spoor of slow-spun earth beneath its own thick coat of grass. Pass through the pillars now, Angus, along the dirt road by the rubble-stone wood shelter on the right and, on the left, an ivy-covered stone wall that fronts the farm-house of whitewashed granite, its lichenous-green slate roof topped with one small decorative gable above the front door and two stone chimneys, one at either end.

The road winds back behind the house up a steep hill past an open, flat-roofed car garage with a lone, wind-bent oak clawing back at the sky above it. Farther along, at the very top of the hill, a grain silo sits on the left and, opposite it, the cow barn where my mother first thrust and then licked me into light. There were three others beside me that morning. One never did move.

Do you recall, did you ever really know it, the full, drowning scent, like wet, rusted iron, of your own birth's blood? How is it that living things can have the smell of metal? Fish. Just today I bit a dead fish on the pond bank behind me here in the woods. Metal!

And the high-pitched taint of that—still on my tongue when, a short time later, I went up to the car that they always park here at the top of the cabin's entrance road, went up to it, why, I think because of the odd angle at which the sun was striking the windshield— that taint on my tongue married perfectly with the fishy one of the car's front bumper.

So tell me, then, where and what do we really come from? Atoms? Adrift? I feel myself going back to them even now, feel the stronger tug, so pleasant, of their desired disassemblage, of me letting go of this shape and, hard on the trail of my own leaking blood, escaping life now on the very same rusty scent that I followed into it.

"An—gus?"

I'm coming. I really do mean to come now. I haven't even one cry of my own left within me, but if I could just get one part of myself to move, I'm certain the rest would follow. They're going to be very frightened when they find me. And then I'll hear those other, different cries.

So many layers and tones it has, the sphere of worry. I've come to know a number of them in the days since I was first taken from Pollard's Combe.

4

A COLD, STORMY DAY IN LATE NOVEMBER, WHEN THE entire sea, it seemed, had mounted England. Air was water and water flowed in raging rivers down the Combe, earthworms flying past me on their way back to earth. By mid-afternoon, the cows—with the help of my mother and Rex, the Border collie—had already been shuttled into the barn. I even got in a few yaps of my own at those perilous hooves.

We were all given some food scraps in the farm-house's back mudroom, where, just before being sent out to the barn with the cows for the night, there were reports from the kitchen radio of towns flooding up and down the Devon and Cornish coast, and of a tanker foundering on the rocks near some place called

Cadgwith, and of a family fishing vessel from the town of Newlyn, lost at sea.

Even I, at all of eight weeks, sensed that this was a night to just hole up somewhere and endure. But there, suddenly, at the farm's edge, a strange, bulbous, blue metal nose with two blinding eyes appeared between the pillars of Pollard's Combe. Watching through the narrow slit in the bottom of the closed barn door, I saw the nose pause out there a moment before slowly bobbing its way up the road, past the woodshed, and the stone wall and house, finally pulling to a stop alongside the back mudroom.

A light went on. The mudroom door opened just as two creaky metal car doors did. And then they—the ones who would change everything—got out and, without any fuss, or argument, were let inside the farmhouse.

Nothing happened, for the longest time. The rain sweeping down. The huddled pod of us shivering out there in the barn. Then the mudroom door opened again, and the owner of Pollard's Combe was coming toward us. I knew, simply by the lean and the rhythm of his gait inside his large overcoat and black rubber boots—the same way he walked out to the barn the day the first one of us disappeared—that something was amiss. He opened the barn door, grabbed me and the other version of me up in his arms, and started back toward the house, my mother following along, head down, behind us.

We were placed down on the mudroom floor. I instantly took to a corner, behind the boiler. The other me—all white but for one brown patch around the left eye—was far more daring. He went toward the intruders, right over to the base of their unfamiliar loom and lean, and looked up: there was the one with the deep voice—a table of shoulders with a huge head rolling around on it—and the other, she of the higher and sweeter sounds, with hands that flew all over as she spoke, like frightened birds trying to get out of the way of the words. Their scents kept mixing in my snout, scents too light, unsoiled, unearthly.

I watched her hands fly down to the floor, clutch the other me, and fly up again. Back and forth he went, tossed in rainstorm torrents of sounds the likes of which I'd not heard before. I don't think the owners of Pollard's Combe had either. I caught a look of their faces, they who never handled us that way, that way which those of you who don't live and work among animals have of holding us up, in an odd, in a, well, a more human light, away from the earth and any practical use.

Holding us up and staring and fondling and staring and letting your speech go all loose and sloppy, and then staring again as though expecting something.

What is it everyone wants so badly? Had I even begun to give it before turning my back on the lights and racing here into the woods?

Would I have given it, eventually, had I stayed, had I not followed my heart, my impulse, here to the dark edge of the forest, but remained, instead, back there in the lighted world, ever vigilant, ever perplexed at the edge of your prolonged, wanting stares?

5

WHERE IS THE OTHER ME NOW? Is he still roaming the grassy hills and high scents of Pollard's Combe? Or did another strange set of headlights appear for him nights later, launch him into his own dizzying tailspin of a life? How close he came to having mine— the steady accretion of concrete, speed, and light that would somehow end at this dark wood's edge.

I was certain he was the one to go that night. They were practically out the door with him, had him there for the longest time in their hands, twisting him into impossible shapes. Then, out of nowhere, here comes his deep voice and huge head, straight toward me. I went under the sink and then behind the boiler again, back and forth, but it was useless, and now I, too, was being handled, discussed, held against his uncertain heart, like a hayloft-trapped starling, and his suddenly certain scent: dried barley and distant bear musk.

He held me to his nose, and then at arm's length, at a dizzying height, and turned me, slowly, like one of those stuffed dogs that the other me probably doesn't even know exist, the ones I've since seen sitting alone on shelves in your rooms, or revolving in city-store windows within the wide sphere of worry.

"It's like choosing a relative," Huge-Head said, carrying me into the kitchen, Sweet-Voice following behind with the other me, my mother waddling over to a corner chair to watch, warily, from a depth of incomprehension that only we can know.

On a long wood table were plates of sickeningly sweet–smelling cakes and tinned biscuits and a pot of tea.

Blab, blab, blab, and blab, and hands flying, and on and on, me, my mother, and the other me straining to hold our heads above the sea-swells of blab.

Why do I hear it now, rising up from those trilling torrents of talk, the story that I would hear again, countless times, in the days that followed, the story they told the owners of Pollard's Combe that night of how they ever came to the gates of their farm and set in motion the dizzying tumble of events that would eventually bring me to this?

They'd gone out the night before, they said, for a few drinks at the Star Inn, in St. Just, the little Cornish village at the far western tip of England where we lived last fall and winter before flying home to this side of the earth; a town of sooty, wet granite and low, off-kilter slate roofs against a wide-open sky; of coal fires, and moss-walled pastures dotted with cows and lone horses, their manes drifting in the stiff sea winds; of misty cliffs riddled with ancient cairns and barrows and the faint, trailing scent of their long-departed spirits.

The Star Inn, a place they'd often take me to, all wrapped up each evening in his jacket, perched against his deep-chested voice and his, by then, knowable heart; looking out as he and Sweet-Voice made their way through the streets to St. Just's main square, more like the rounded, teat-swelled belly of a nursing bitch, people pulling at the different doors of all the scent-filled shops.

A short ways off the square was the entrance to the inn, two fat, foot-worn stone steps up into a low-lit, curtained bear cave of a room with black-lacquered rafters, and a fire flickering within one wall. The other walls, and the ceiling, too, were decked with pieces of old sunken ships and strange glass-framed squares of withered fish stiffly aswim in dusty, waterless seas.

Head-tilt.

They took their usual place at the end of the bar. They had no intention, they said, of getting another me. Already had one back home, a Dalmatian named Lucy, who they had to leave behind for the six months they were away because she was too old to make the journey.

But, somehow, the conversation turns to Jack Russell terriers. Sweet-Voice says she's always wanted one, and suddenly he's asking the pub tender—"laconic," is what she's always called him—he's asking Mr. Laconic what he knows about Jack Russell terriers, and if there are any breeders in the area.

The tender leans over. I can still see him, a big, round, white face, not enough blood in it. He shakes his head. Doesn't know a thing about it, then walks off to the back room behind the bar to let out his own terrier, a mixed breed who always slept in the cushioned basket under the bar and regarded me with complete disinterest.

The whole discussion might have ended right there and my life at the Combe have been left alone to go on as it had been, me in the barn, nudged up against warm tummy, teat, and straw. But I know them, my new masters, how they can go on and on about a thing once they've gotten it in their minds, the way I like to turn a killed mouse over and over to divine every fold of its stink.

They sat there at the bar, going back and forth, about the pros and cons of my breed, about how particularly devilish they'd heard Jack Russells can be, so stubborn and willful. They talked about the problem of transporting a me back here to this side of the world (an ordeal which, now that I've been through it, I don't think they could have possibly given enough thought to) and about whether or not I would be a good thing for Lucy. They weighed, they said, all the bad and the good points, counting among the latter the fact that they're both writers and home all day and still have no kids to deal with, and surely Lucy would love to have a companion to keep her active and lively in her waning years.

On and on they went in the Pollard's Combe kitchen that night, even my worry-sick mother dosing in her corner chair. The other me looked numbed by the kneading of Sweet-Voice's hands, while I, weakening under the weight of all the words and the foul sweetness of those kitchen-table cakes, finally stopped wriggling in Huge-Head's arms, decided to go even further into them and feel the vibrations of his voice, and the slow, plodding pace of the human heart as it decides another creature's fate.

Thrust of chance. Arbitrary pendulum swings.

It was, they said, just as they were coming to their senses—just as they were deciding that a dog like me would be too much to take on at this point in their lives—that Mr. Laconic returned with that week's edition of *The Cornishman*, put it, without a word, down on the bar, pointed to the item on the classified page that read, TWO JACK RUSSELL TERRIER PUPPIES. The very next night, the headlights appeared between the entrance pillars of Pollard's Combe.

"It's like choosing a relative," Huge-Head said again.

"Take them both," Mr. Pollard said.

"Yes," Sweet-Voice answered, and I could feel Huge-Head's heart go a little faster.

There was a long silence, and then Sweet-Voice suddenly announced that she saw something in the way I looked there in his arms, a twinkle, a certain vigor.

"Yes. Me too," he said. "I've warmed to him, too."

He stood up, held and turned me again for a good long look, then turned to see my mother's head shifting back and forth with his every movement.

"She hates us," he said. "She knows we're taking her baby away."

What are we, I wonder, that we have, like you, deep emotions and yet can't ever really live up to the notions you have of us? As if my mother, and I, and the other me had a set of hopes and dreams that were about to be arrested there that night, a set of expectations beyond our immediate wish that we might all be returned to the barn in order to pull close together again and ride out the rest of that night's storm.

What are we that we don't live up to your notions and yet end up living entirely for you?

Can you imagine, have you ever known anything like it at all, the feeling of being torn from your own mother's side and then, in a matter of days, becoming so fiercely devoted to the very ones who took you away that you'd attack anything that threatened them? That you would, on a night just like this one, at the mere suggestion of a threatening scent, desert the very comfort they had made for you and charge off blindly here to the dark wood's edge?

Do we have hearts like yours, hearts that can be broken beyond the immediate pain, like a deep bite, that was felt—you could see it in my mother's eyes—when they did, at last, stand and announce that I, nameless as yet, was to be the one?

He handed me to Sweet-Voice—creamy wheat with

a phantom waft of wild onion grass—turned and put sixty pounds in Farmer Pollard's hand, and it was done. Just like that, we were leaving, me staring out from the folds of her coat, watching the other me recede into the shadows of the mudroom, watching my mother watch me go forever out the door.

But if you asked how many days has my mother thought of me since, or I, before this night, of her, what should I tell you? Who deemed that we should feel so deeply the very things that we'll never think upon again? That we be the dimmer ones who live so much more fiercely than you do? We, who bound from one evaporative day to the next, reading each day's scents and threats so that you can idly pass their hours, staring back out at us from the well-guarded confines of your comfort, reading into us all the things you believe we must think and feel and dream.

I think this: devotion needs not memory but doggedness. The ability to dig up and then bury each day, like a bone, one after the next, with no notion of past or future days, with no idea that the sum of all those bones adds up to something called a life.

Do you know, have you ever heard the story of my fellow terrier, a Skye terrier named Bobby? All dogs have. All dogs know about other dogs, know them in our bones.

Abandoned and starving on the streets of Edinburgh, Scotland, Bobby was found and taken in by a kindly police constable. He immediately took to following the constable everywhere in the course of his daily rounds, went with him even to his noonday lunch at Ramsay's Inn, where he'd get each day from his master's plate a gravy-soaked bun.

Years of these day-bones accrued and then the constable died. Bobby was at the funeral and remained there at the churchyard long after everyone left, refusing to go, even with those who tried to offer him a new home. The following day, at noon sharp, he showed up at Ramsay's Inn, where a familiar patron offered him up his usual gravy-soaked bun.

Bobby took it in his mouth and ran back to the churchyard to eat. He would do the same, each day, one after the other, for the next nine years, until the day he finally felt the tug of his own atoms' desired dismissal from this world and followed them into the ground right there alongside the constable's grave.

So who and what are we really, then, and have we, would you say, hearts like yours?

6

Scent. Rising. Growing stronger. They're coming back to finish me off. Why didn't they before?

"An—gus?"

Cries. Theirs.

Are they what first scared the fangs away, the fangs of the coyotes? How many of them were there? Two had me in their jaws, I think. From the front and back. There was some twisting.

"An—gus?"

The scent, falling away now, back into the forest.

"An—gus?" Thin, high-pitched, sweet, her cries, vaguely singsong, relaxed, friendly.

They still have no idea.

I can, if I lift my head now away from the ruined rest of me, just barely see, beyond these trees, and above the tops of the uncut hay fronds, the blurred outline of her.

I'm very fond of her, aren't I? I am "more hers." She's always saying that, and I suppose it's so, but her hands, they were a big problem for me at first, too needy and delicate, dancing all the time up and down my length, trying to mold me into her lap.

I'm no lap dog. I'm a terrier. "Terra." I'm of the earth. I tear at it, was born to work it, to pull animals from their burrows, to charge across and fall, and sleep upon the earth. My days were the deadly shuffle of cow hooves and roaring tractor tread, swinging teats and milk-spray and big ripe mounds of shit.

Even at eight weeks, I was charging up over the hill at the Combe to the back fields for the hunt, watching my mother maul rats, field mice, moles, the occasional fox or badger, and then getting to visit day after day in secret with the withering carcass and the gathering dimensions of its scent.

My life was an ever-shifting sea of scents, stirring, suddenly, up, like those rain squalls off the cliffs of St. Just, so many that I'd often have to stop, throw my head back, and, with a pair of nostrils poised just above the drowning rest of me, hang on to dear life by each of the Combe's passing essences: rot, molder, and manure; the dense punch of newly plowed pastures; the thin, gauzy thread of just harvested ones.

There were endless air-etched rivulets of scent to travel down: earthworm-moist and butterfly-dust; hoof-hollow, paw-pads, and seagull swill; and all of these trails subsumed in the end by that wider, base-note scent of my life at the Combe: teat, tummy, and straw, lightly baked by a day-long, drowsy sun.

You've known these, too, haven't you, days adrift in shifting scents, without reflection?

"Ang—us? . . ."

Where am I now? Have I moved at all? I can't see Sweet-Voice anymore, only the distant yellow glow of the cabin lights, warm, full, against all that hilltop darkness.

What have I done? What wasn't I thinking? I remember so little. Just that scent, rising, and the feel of charging toward it, and then the flash of fangs and the swirl of lights, and me, here, hard on the trail of my own leaking blood.

"Ang—us? . . ."

There she is.

"Ang-us!"

Do you hear it, the difference? How the first cry has that upward-rising, inquisitive beat.

That's the early-evening cry, the one they began to sound a short while ago, looking for me the way they have every night here, in the twilight, when that fear boundary of theirs hasn't quite formed yet, and they're still friendly toward me because they're certain I'm fine.

Night after night this summer—the first of what they were hoping to be many with me—we've gone through this. I'm out here somewhere under the stars, on the dark earth, looking for moving things.

Did I tell you this, why we're always chewing up and ripping your belongings? Why we often run through your rooms in senseless circles and can stare forever at spinning flywheels or even a silly pair of your hands fluttering as you talk, like frightened birds trying to get out of the way? It's because to us your world just lies there. Doesn't do enough.

Each night I've run off like this, past twilight, but not very far. There's usually enough moving here just on the other side of that fear boundary that seems to grow more defined for you as the hours pass, and darkness falls, and then I hear that other cry, quick, downbeat, edgy: "An-gus!" bidding me look back, once or twice, over my shoulder, at their ridiculous shadows tensed within the outer glow of the cabin lights, barely leaning into the open field, leaning just past their fears, for some indication of me.

And each night I've come back. I've always come back. It's been this way from the start. From our very first days in England together, the three of us out along the far western cliffs of Cornwall, where the earth roves like a ship's prow through the sea, and me—all eleven weeks and five pounds of me—running ahead, going out to the very cliff's edge, poised there, earth's tiny, animate bowsprit, staring into mist, feeling it, the drift of disassembled matter, the taste and trail of the scent that leads nowhere.

I'd hear them calling to me from somewhere far behind in the mist, "An—gus?" "An—gus?" one voice deep, the other, higher and thin, but I'd go on, go to the very farthest tendrils of their cries. I wouldn't stop until the path came to the Ballowall Barrow, that massive circle of stones built by the ancient men high on the clifftop overlooking nothing but ocean and air.

Inside it, there was a small, tight circular path that led to the rooms where the ancient men would lay their dead, rooms we'd often have to take cover in when those sudden squalls of rain would sweep in, sideways, from the sea. The three of us huddled there in silence, dripping, thrilled—weren't we thrilled?—as cold rain lashed the stones, and the wind drew long, piercing howls from the spiny gorse shrubs, and kept ripping away their brief, yellow-flowered fragrance, mixing it with the body of that deeper, timeless scent in which we were all huddled there.

Can you recall it? Did you ever know it? A scent beyond moss, and rock and brine, beyond time, a scent both primordial and new, whose trail leads nowhere?

They must have known it, those ancient stone builders, placing their dead there, as close as they could get them on the earth to land's end, where matter drifts and limits lift; where even they, my new masters, found themselves, leaning to see what's around the next bend.

Where am I now?

It's so quiet.

Everything is quiet again but for the peepers and the seething stars. I see the cabin. They must be back inside, sitting up there together, where I would normally be by now, lying alongside them amidst the sudden, violent blue flashes of that little glass room they hauled all the way up here from our city rooms, the flashing box with the warm, bitter smell wafting up from the back of the lighted day inside.

They've stopped worrying about me. I've done this too many nights before, they're thinking, and I'm always fine. I always come back.

And soon, when and if they do ever find me, they'll be going over and over it in their minds, doubting themselves, hearing those voices, the what-if's and second-guesses, asking why they didn't try to call me sooner, why they let me out alone so late, allowing me to do what I had to: charge, in spite of everything, toward the heart of this moving forest to which pure chance brought me.

"He's gone too far this time," I can already hear them saying. "Met his match." "Overstepped his bounds." "Obeyed his instincts in a place where there are forces far more powerful than anything he might have come up against in Devon, England," my fully tamed and tilled native England, the badgers and the foxes, the very creatures that I was destined to spend my life pulling from their holes in the earth around Pollard's Combe until they, my new masters, showed up there and changed all that. Until they arrived that stormy night last November and pulled me from my purpose.

The whole drive home to St. Just, her hands kept pressing, kept needing me. They, as much as the motion of the car, are what made me so sick.

Where does it come from, such depth of need?

What is it you want?

Have I given it?

So many layers and tones it has, your world.

7

Sixty pounds was paid, and suddenly I'm going along, without question, for the ride of my life. Time of journey? I have no notion of such things, but clearly long enough to change my days forever. That's the way of creatures like me, the simpler ones, the dim relatives with the ever-bright dispositions, we, who go, without too much fuss, wherever fate and the thrust of chance leads us.

I lay in her lap, the car bobbing like a drunken boat through that night of squalls and drowning villages, and narrow, hedgerowed lanes. For a time the road grew wider and straight. The world flew faster and more smoothly by, and the car settled into something constant and calm, and I remember the two of them began to talk.

They talked of me mostly and of the life they would have with me and Lucy when we all got home to her, and how thrilled she'd be to have a companion in her old age. They talked of needing to buy books about Jack Russell terriers in order to learn how best to handle the likes of my breed, my singular, storied breed.

And then, even as we were hurtling along that rainy night, further and further into the choice they'd finally made, and the life that we were bound upon together, he suddenly began to wonder if they shouldn't have chosen the other me.

He reached over with a free hand, joined it with her meddlesome two atop and along my head and flank, and started talking about the other me with the one brown eye patch and wasn't he so adorable, and unique, and so much like some dog he'd seen on TV as a kid.

"I can't believe we took this one," he said. "Why did we take this one?"

"I don't know," she said. "I just started to fall in love with him, the way he looked there in your arms."

"Yes," he answered, "when he was sitting in my arms at the table. Something about him. But the other one. What a face."

"I love this face," she said, a little angry now. "The other one was too runty, too aggressive. And I didn't like the sound of his breathing."

"This one does have the two black eye patches. That's really the classic Jack Russell face, isn't it?"

He went on this way for much of the ride, talking about what might have been, indulging an urge—much like my own to dig and dig—to picture, to practically reside within a way things could have gone had he made a different choice, even as he was driving us ever further into the consequences of the one he had.

There must be some use for it, your regret, like the soothing to and fro of the wipers that night across our drowning windshield of trickling stars.

I lay there in her lap, my eyes drifting open and closed, the car speeding me forever away from teat, tummy, and straw. I lay there listening to it, the sound of regret, of misgiving, giving me sleep.

8

"AN — GUS?"

His cry now. Singsong still.

Keep going, Angus.

The car came to rest at last that night in the rain between a blue door and the open sea. Number twenty-two, Bosorne Road, the last in a row of two-story, granite cottages lining a narrow, dead-end lane, a lumpy, hedgerowed pasture directly across from us.

We got out of the car, me wrapped in her coat, the rain still sweeping down. The blue door opened. We all went in. Of rooms I'd known only the barn at Pollard's Combe and the mudroom, and, for as long as it took to be chosen and bought that night, the brashly lit kitchen.

Go in, Angus. Go back there now, the first in a long

series of rooms that you'd pass through before finally arriving here, to the end of rooms, on the far side of fear, in the dark, in the moving world.

To my immediate right was a squeezed set of stairs shooting straight up into darkness. Very frightening. Directly ahead, a living room, nothing much, two ratty sofas, one beneath the heavily draped front window, the other positioned across from it, a small coal stove set in between them against the far wall. A table stood against the wall beneath the stairs. A glass door at the back opened onto a closet-sized kitchen, and another door off of it led back out to the open night again.

I remember it all now. The place where we began together. Or, I should say, the place where I began, however tentatively, to devote all my attentions to them, to herd all of my instincts into the vacated corrals of theirs, into rooms, anonymous rooms.

"Put him down," he said.

And I went drowsily about, sizing up the looming presences within, the furniture you seem all too trusting of, so certain that it will stay in place and be there by morning: table, sofa, stove, end table, things we sniff and bite merely because they seem to be holding out on us, to have other schemes.

I went behind all the furniture, went under and around it, eavesdropping on the ongoing, silent revolt of objects.

And then I went into the unfurnished, the room's forgotten, quadrants, the spaces orphaned by your designs, sniffing out wraiths, absorbing disquiet, knowing no hierarchy of air, no best place in the room to be; knowing in my bones that nothing is what it appears, that objects, too, ache, the way that all atom-arrangements do, for disassemblage.

Passing into the kitchen, I came to the back door. Huge-Head opened it. Let me out into a walled-in backyard no larger than a couple of cows.

A walled-in yard.

Odd thing to do, odd thing to do.

Look up, Angus. I saw a cloud streaked moon, bleeding in a corner of night.

White plastic chairs lay on their side in the grass beside the lopped-off basin of a birdbath. Wedged against one wall was the briefest man-made, half-moon pond, the bottom lined with black plastic.

The rain had stopped by then. An icy wind blew the pond's moonlit surface into snarls. I sniffed them. Just then a goldfish rose, regarded me, retreated into the murk. Then another. They were down there. Dormant. Alive. Down in the dark room of the standing water, going on, undevoted, nameless.

I remember now. This was my last moment on earth without a name, a creature as yet uncallable, more closely aligned with those starving, pond-blind goldfish than with my new owners: the two of them sitting inside the cottage, trying to decide on my name, that simple, two-beat tug on the spirit, on the heart, a sound as high and as formidable to me now as the walls that bound me there that first night.

"An—gus?"

Singsong still.

What is Angus?

What am I without that two-beat tug on my heart?

Go back now, Angus, toward your own nameless-ness, to the time before they arrived and sped you off to Cornwall and then to the dizzying spires of cemented scent and light that would become your life until they brought you here—a life of appointed rounds and worn-down paw-pads on sidewalks; of long, droning hours high up in the furnished city cells, napping on sofas, and going to the windows to stare out over the ongoing frets of black rooftops and siren-laced streets; of going back and forth all day between Huge-Head and Sweet-Voice, each of them working in their own rooms, sitting upright, motionless, only their hands clacking in front of lit glass boxes where rows of tiny black birds keep alighting and flying off and then seettling back down again.

Go back past that night, that endless night of your passage from England to this side of the world, locked in a tiny crate and conveyed, slowly, into the shiny underbelly of a vast metal bird. Me, all five or so pounds of me, alive within the belly of the bird that suddenly rumbled up off the earth and roared through space, fast, furious, and farther and on and on, with a whole barnyard of crated creatures stacked there around me— emu, parrots, llamas, horses, and one rhinoceros, battling his sedatives, slowly swaying his heavy head—the whole lot of us up there, one room beneath the humans, going along for them with the ride.

Go back to Devon, Angus, through the pillars of Pollard's Combe, and along the road behind the farmhouse to the sky-clawing oak and the days of high scents and the barn of your birth. Enter through the barn doors again, into the wafts of teat, tummy, and straw, and, hard on the trail of your own mother's warm milk and blood, pass out of daylight back inward toward your own beginning, involute, devolving, and on and on, back to when you, too, were a nameless, pond-blind little fish aswim in the murk.

"At the end of May, in the year 1819 . . ."

Where did I hear this?

I remember.

Huge-Head was reading it aloud to Sweet-Voice just the other day from one of his dog books; the two of them sitting as they do every evening here at the top of this field beside the silver birch and the stone cooking pit; sitting there by the fire as I went about my business, rummaging through the field of tansy and goldenrod behind the fire pit, tearing the guts from one of the snakes I'd just killed.

"At the end of May, in the year 1819, when strolling round Magdalen Meadow with Horace in hand . . . Reverend Russell emerged from the classic shade of Addison's Walk, crossed the Cherwell in a punt, and passed over in the direction of Marston, hoping to devote an hour or two to study in the quiet meads of that hamlet, near the charming slopes of Elsfield, or in the deeper and more secluded haunts of Shotover Wood. Before he had reached Marston, a milkman met him with a terrier—such an animal as Russell had yet seen only in his dreams; he halted, as Acteon might have done when he caught sight of Diana desporting in her bath; but unlike that ill-fated hunter, he never budged from the spot till he had won the prize and secured it for his own. She was called Trump, and became the progenitress of that famous race of terriers which, from that day to the present, have been associated with Russell's name at home and abroad. . . ."

Head-tilt.

Trump? As lovely as Diana? Whose dog was she? Trump. One-beat tug. Trump. My original, my first mother, taken from a man made of milk by a Reverend with a dog named Horace, two-beat tug, and small, like me, it seems, if he could fit in a hand.

Horace and Trump. Were they my beginnings?

Huge-Head called me to his side that night by the fire. He held a picture up to my nose, kept pointing at it, repeating, "Trump."

Head-tilt.

Pictures mean nothing to us, small openings into days where nothing moves, nothing ever changes. But I see the image clearly now: a me, mostly white with a dark patch over each eye and ear, exactly like mine, though my right ear does have a stray stretch of white running up the back. There's the same titch of brown at the base of the tail. The same coarse, wiry coat that I've begun to develop in recent months. The same tense, alert posture that trusts no one or thing.

How long did it take the Reverend to concoct a me? "The good country parson," Huge-Head called him, "who divided his days between a love of God and terriers . . . A spiritual man with a passion for the earthly hunt."

How long to arrive at a me, the fierce tagalong of your passions; "hard-bitten little souls," as the Reverend called us, "with a particularly blunt view of pain;" that perfect blend of devotion and recklessness that would leave me no choice but to charge out here tonight. Not on a whim, not for my own delight, but to challenge a part of my own nameless ancestry, the ones who never came along for the ride; challenge them because they had strayed too close to that fear boundary I've learned to guard just as I have all the other rooms I've been introduced to in the sphere of worry, with their unquiet spirits, scheming furniture, and orphaned air.

Will they know this, my masters, when they think back on this night, know that I had no choice? Will they, when and if they do ever find me, understand that I did this for them?

Go back now, Angus, if only a little bit ago, to the moment of the rising scent and the headlong charge.

A moment that was, at one time, all of the time, when it was me or the likes of me and of the very ones who felled me tonight, out together roaming in packs the world ongoing and nameless. The distant time before we began to prey about the edges of your lights, and fears, and names; before we began to be rewarded for guarding and providing for these; for returning, as I'm trying to now, to these. A time that has since become a broken-off remnant and yet one that I was still, finally, too small and tame for; too much of this world and of my bond with them, the ones who sit up there now within the warm glow and violent blue flashes of the cabin lights.

"An—gus?"

Cries. Theirs.

Here.

He is here. Is me. I am Angus. Two-beat tug. Nothing more. I am what you've made me, the one who would do over and over again what I've done tonight, the one who won't find himself again until he's found his way back to you.

"An—gus?"

They sound much clearer now.

Could I be coming closer even as I feel myself fading away, drifting toward my own end?

If only they could come a bit farther down, come fully out into this side field of darkness and the magnet-like wobble of resistance that I can feel building now between their minds and this wood.

If only they had my eyes, which gather all the night's ambient light, they might see me, or see, at least, the hay fronds slowly bend and sway above me as I crawl.

Angus! Angus! Angus! They kept saying my new name that first night in Cornwall when they came back out into the walled yard. Over and over until they saw my head begin to tilt to it. Until it started to tug at my heart, and I was firmly hooked: another feisty tagalong through your world of names.

"Lu—cy?" "Lu—na?" "Fran—cis?" "Smoke—y?" "Bru—no?" "Cha—os?" and on and on, all the dogs I've met in these past months, all the broken-off pieces of my former packs, running now with yours, guarding and completing and returning, faithfully, to yours.

"Angelly Spangelly." "Little Shit." "The Bugger." "Dockside-Tough-In-A-Tight-White-T." "Mister-I-Met-A-Man." I've been called all of these. I have been held up in any number of odd lights, shaken before gritted teeth, and bit lips, and called, for whatever reason, these.

"Angelly Spangelly . . . Ang—gang—ga—Spangelly." I've had this sung to me, as well; have tilted my head at this and far more baffling displays, Huge-Head or Sweet-Voice or the both of them, my masters, singing that senseless tune, over and over, prancing around the St. Just cottage, or through the rooms of our various city cells, or right up there in the cabin, singing that and countless other oddities; and me all the while watching them, thinking that maybe sometimes the world doesn't move enough for you either.

9

Tuh-rump, tuh-rump, tuh-rump, tuh-rump, tuh-rump, tuh-rump, tuuuuhhhhhh—rump: me, all five pounds of me, dashing back up the Cornwall cottage stairs at the end of my morning housebreaking sessions and then, with one flat-out, full-length dive, plopping down again into the cloud of blankets and bed sheets still being warmed by Huge Old Lazy Head against the late-November, bone-damp chill.

He'd wait up there in bed just for me, for the joy of my reckless return, and I, I'm sure of it now, couldn't wait to deliver it to him. Long after Sweet-Voice had roused and carried me downstairs to teach me of yet another of your boundaries, the one between things done inside and things done out, he'd be waiting up there under the covers like a big toothless badger.

What had come over me? Just days after being swiped from the sweet scents and hard certainties of the Combe, there I was, charging headlong into the wilds of domesticity: hierarchies of air, the sweet spots in rooms, window views, preyless pleasures.

Huge-Head would wallow away the better part of the morning, and I'd burrow into that, into the curious depth of his capacity for delay, as enticing as any hunt across the Devon countryside. I can be very determined, have spent hours here in these very woods at the base of trees that I've chased a porcupine or a raccoon up. But to linger at the root of an empty bough, to merely linger, this was truly unknown terrain.

He'd loll, and I—fierce tagalong even of tarrying—lolled with him. I even learned some things, things entirely useless to a me, but things nonetheless. Each morning, for instance, the same two horses came along the sea road, just beneath our sill, not work horses like the ones at Pollard's Combe, and not those trained for the hunt, but pleasure horses, being taken out for a ride: two felt-capped human heads bobbing past us atop loud, smelly, slow-leaking sacks of clip-clops.

We'd stay up there together for quite some time,

Huge-Head and me. From downstairs, Sweet-Voice would occasionally call over the rim of her tea cup: "Ain't you ever gettin' up, boss?" and he'd grumble and grab and turn me over and further into him, his eyes closed, mine stuck wide, wondering how far an idle pursuit such as this can be taken.

I'd hear cowbells in the distance, fog-muffled, adrift. And tractor snarls, but groundless, as though plowing air, great flocks of seagulls laughing in their wake. It was as if all the tenets of my former life had been loosed from their moorings, the Combe's old alignment of scent, earth, and toil unraveled.

Perching myself up on my back legs, front paws resting on the windowsill, I was just big enough to see out across Bosorne Road and the grass-mounded hedgerow bordering the pasture opposite our front door. The cows would already be out, and with no prodding from me, no work or danger for me. A herd of harmless, fat, spotted dreams, grazing.

I'd begin to wriggle away. Pull at the covers. Pick up chew toys and drop them, one by one, into that room's widening maw of inaction, trying either to fill or choke it. But he'd go even further in, make me attend, make me watch him. He'd turn himself over, close his eyes, open them, stare straight up, blow air softly from his mouth, say things. Water, sometimes, would suddenly gather about the corner of his lids, spill over. I'd lick it for the salt.

What is it you want? What is it that you're always hunting for in the air? Where could its burrow be? Can I help you find it?

The day really didn't pick up much when Huge-Head finally did get out of bed. He'd go downstairs, put on his overcoat, tie a leash to my neck, step out the blue front door, place me down on Bosorne Road, and start toward the village center only to be yanked backward by me, all five pounds or so of me.

I lead. Always. I have no say in this. It's in my atoms. Huge-Head would try dragging me along, drag me until my paws burned. Then he'd stop, reach down, put me in his coat and walk.

Town, I learned soon enough, was just more rooms, winding blocks of rooms and flocks of strange hands coming down on my head amidst high, fluttering voices—everyone in England, it seems, having a tale about a Jack Russell terrier, what amazing little me's we are.

"Two were found not long ago," I can remember a woman at the bread room saying one morning as she patted my head. "They were abandoned, shivering, on the streets of a town called Averley. One had been stabbed by his former owner in the eyes, which had to be removed and sewn shut. The poor darlings were taken to the local pound and, as God is my witness, the one with the good eyes soon took to leading the other one around by the scruff of his neck, taking him to all corners of the yard until he got the lay of the place.

"Wasn't long after that," she continued, squeezing my snout in her hands, "that the little darlings were adopted by a wealthy family in Brighton. Bill. They named the blind one Bill, and the other Ben, and he leads Bill everywhere now, from room to room, and through a spacious back garden and later to bed, the two of them sleeping together each night intertwined in a basket."

Those mornings in St. Just, we'd go, old Huge-Head and I, all through town, from the newspaper room, to the bread room, to the room with the meat and the eggs, and the one with the vegetables, and the one where he got the bottle of dark brown, nostril-piercing liquid that he always brought out in the evening at the cottage and that, well, changed things, made even the room's orphaned air feel more at home.

Satchels in arm, me perched at his sternum, we'd

then wind our way back home to Bosorne Road and the deeply unmoving hours of Huge-Head and Sweet-Voice's workday.

Back and forth I'd go between them, trying to get the exact lay of my new life, which, as far as I could make out, required of me only that I be there.

Huge-Head sat upstairs in a small room just off the one with the bed in it, his desk set under a window with a distant view over the walled backyard of pond-blind goldfish to the wide-open sea. Sweet-Voice worked downstairs on the sofa beside the coal stove, her lit square of alighting birds set in her lap.

The better part of the day I spent with her, because she sits still less well than he, gets up more often, does things other than stare off blankly, things closer to my heart like eating, and hunting for new things to eat, and thinking about what might be good to eat later, and preparing it.

Her days, too, are sensory onslaughts, of textures and touch. She's restless, like me, impatient in her bones. She senses the unseen, the about-to-happen, and knows, I'm certain of it, about the way of atoms and the path of souls. She's told him from the very beginning that I am more her dog, and though he always takes it the wrong way, I know what she means.

Early afternoons, more nothingness loomed, but I at least got to go stir crazy within the lingering odors of lunch, and the fading memory of the scraps that had been tossed down to me from the table or the kitchen sink during cleanup.

Afterward, Huge-Head would carry me out into the walled yard, set me down in the grass, stand there, waiting. I'd look up at him. He'd turn away. He'd look back down. I'd turn, then start back toward the kitchen door.

"Angus . . ." he'd call, and then he'd make his voice go strangely deep and round: "No!"—a tiny word that he made sound like a dark, bottomless well I'd never climb out of if I took another step.

"Nooooo!"

He'd have to walk over, pick me up, and put me back in the grass. We'd repeat this dim little dance three or four times, do it day after day, until that afternoon when, having sniffed every blade of grass, every inch of wall, and plastic pond shore; having exhausted every possible guess at what it was he was standing there waiting for me to do—I squatted and relieved myself. A simple, unavoidable outcome, and yet one that unleashed such a torrent of praise and sweet biscuits, I saw no reason not to repeat it from that day forward.

Back inside, Huge-Head would go upstairs again to his desk. Sweet-Voice would sit on the sofa by the lighted coal stove, writing in her journal. The day droned on, the only suggestion of the outside world being the oily essence of the coal chunks I'd chew beneath the stove, and, at about midafternoon—sandwiched in between the gather and fade of someone's footsteps on the road out front—a brief flash of light that would open in the blue door, letting a bunch of envelopes drop through to the floor.

Sweet-Voice would go over, pick them up, open them.

"Here's another from Lucy," she'd often say, and then read it to me, a letter written in Lucy's voice by the women who were taking care of her back here on this side of the world.

Head-tilt.

My time would finally come in the late afternoon. Once outside the blue door, we'd turn left on Bosorne Road and follow its tall, mossy hedgerows past England's last walled pasture before the open sea, two cloaked and riderless horses standing there, motionless, but for the sea winds fingering their manes.

Bosorne Road wound down into Cott's Valley, became a narrow footpath at the base of steep, russet-colored hillsides, dotted here and there with heather and gorse, the ocean's wavy, hackle-raised back rising up at the valley's far end, one lunge, it seemed, from swallowing us and the earth whole. I'd go right up to it. Into the gut-hollowing roar of its rock-launched mists.

"An—gus?" "An—gus?" I'd hear, calling me back, calling me away from the very place I find myself now—far beyond rooms, at the edge of where the limits lift and the end comes around again to the beginning.

"An—gus?" they'd call, and then "An-gus!" the sharp, the edgy cry, that would only drive me farther on. This was my time.

Up the cliff face I'd lead them, all along the edges, high above the sea, "An—gus?" "An-gus!" past the Barrow and the rooms of the ones who knew of the path of souls. Here and there out above the ocean, those gray snags of rainy air would gather and charge and come collapsing down upon us, leaving us huddled up behind some stone, or in the rooms of the ancient men, drenched and thrilled.

One day, I led us along a steep cliff face, down among the shore rocks to visit a sea lion perched there on a rock amidst the crashing waves, like a big, proud, sea-borne me whose legs the ocean had long ago abraded. We got close enough for me to catch his scent—a warm briny slather of metallic sea-berry and salt—before he plunged into the waves, drawing our eyes outward to the huge squall gathering there against the horizon.

We started climbing back up, but it was already too late, was coming too fast. I stopped in my tracks—every atom said to—and for the first time in my life, watched them take the lead, race ahead. They were already near the top of the cliff before they realized. I heard her screaming at him to stop, to turn back, just as the first gales of icy rain slashed across, taking her voice away, taking the breath from their mouths.

I turned inward, nestled into a tiny nook in the cliff face, shivered there like a winged gull, still smelling the last traces of that sea lion, far off by then, sliding seamlessly through the deep. Above me, the two of them were backing their way along the ledge together, taking air from the inside of their coats, his outstretched arm letting the whole of her down, bit by bit, toward me, just the one of those two needy hands of hers, grasping.

I kept ducking it. I don't know why. "AN-GUS!!" After a number of swipes, she finally got hold of that floppy, extra bit of me at the back of the neck—the part my mother used to swing us around Pollard's Combe by—and in one sweeping arc, I was passed from her to him and the broad, warming wall of his chest.

Blab, blab, blab, and on and on they went all the way back to the cottage—the sun washing over Cott's Valley as suddenly as the rains had—the two of them talking to each other about what a close one that was; about how I'd really bitten off more than I could chew that time, me wriggling in his coat all the while to get down and take the lead again.

Back at the cottage, I took up residence with the wet socks and shoes by the warmth of the coal stove, far away from the flaming tongues of my new masters, tongues stoked by that bottled brown liquid, the two of them telling and retelling the events of that afternoon, of our "close one," turning it over and over again, the details gathering dimension just like the stink of one of my conquered carcasses. The height of the cliff, the bite of the storm, the depth of their fear.

The whole thing carried over to the Star Inn, to our nightly visit there, the place in which my fate was first sealed. Huge-Head cradled me against him the entire night, afraid to let me out of his sight, my head swimming in the smoke and the fumes of the brown liquid. Mr. Laconic, his big bowed arms resting on clenched fists against the bar, a white towel over one shoulder, listened amidst the fluttering of hands and the rising voices to the tale of how the "Little Shit" he'd helped them find almost got them killed today. He stood there slowly shaking his round, bloodless face at me.

"An—gus?" "An—gus?"

There they are again.

Will I ever get back to them, ever get to hear those wild tongues again; hear them tell and retell the tale of this night, and all the ways it will grow: how I fought off an entire pack of coyotes; how I crawled back miles and miles to reach home; the tales of deeds and of day-bones we'd never dig up again.

I remember now being borne home that night through St. Just's narrow, drizzled streets, my back pressed to Huge-Head's heart, my head aswivel, watching her listen to him, him to her. Watching the low, clustered tilt of rooftops against the ongoing sky. A few window lights blinked off. The whole town dipped and swayed as we walked.

To keep from being sick, I kept one eye out for our blue door. As much as I hated the drone of the hours we spent behind it, I was quietly, inwardly, willing us back home to them.

I did learn things there, a whole new landscape of pointless hunts: the shameless thrill of flying headlong into a soft bed; of padding about upon a human back; of nipping lightly at a sleeping ear. I discovered that in a pinch the nook of a neck will briefly satisfy any burrowing instinct.

I learned—whenever they went out, and I was left alone in that narrow cottage with the stairs to the bedroom barricaded, and the door to the kitchen locked, and the thick, muffled sounds of those backyard goldfish turning in my ears—to attack all furniture, piss on its legs. I learned to chew to pieces those thick, stinky shadows of traitorous human feet known as shoes.

All out of anxiety, not vengeance. We aren't capable of revenge. Didn't you know this? Your province again. No matter how deep your slights and betrayals, we can only gnaw away—as a wild animal does the limb it catches in one of your traps—at our own fear of never being returned to again.

I learned that your world is full of holes, burrows of all sizes, shapes, and directions, up or down, whose prey may never be found, or out-waited.

I learned that days can sometimes grow too heavy to bear, and yet they'll keep arriving, one after the other, whether it's the earth of them you like to dig in, or the air.

10

WE WERE SITTING IN THE LIVING ROOM OF THE
Bosorne Road cottage, Sweet-Voice and me.

Why am I remembering this?

Huge-Head was upstairs napping. She was reading
on the sofa. I was at her feet, chewing a chunk of coal.
Outside, another day of dense mist and rain pressed in
at our windows.

Sweet-Voice stood up, went to the kitchen.

"A nice cup of tea, eh, Angelly?"

I followed her. You never know when a tidbit is
going to fall your way. She stood by the sink, watching
out the back window, waiting for her water to start bub-
bling, her stockinged feet taking turns resting on each
other. Then she reached toward the shelf above the

sink, and flipped a switch: voices like the ones from the kitchen radio at the Combe.

I went and got my coal chunk, brought it back and dropped it on her top foot with a slather of saliva. Just to see what she would do. She reached down, lifted me up, held my nose to hers.

"Mister . . ." she said, biting her bottom lip, "I'm tryin' to listen to this."

Head-tilt.

She kept me there in her arms. I tried to wriggle away, then rested my head on her shoulder, staring out into the day, into the folding, ever-shifting textures of the mist.

"And what should we say," a voice asked, "when we are able to talk with them?"

"I think the first thing we should tell them is how sorry we are for all the centuries of misunderstanding."

Blab, blab, blab, and on and on.

I turned, saw Sweet-Voice's head tilt.

"Oh my God, Spangelly. They're talking about you. Shhhh!"

"It is my understanding," the first voice said, "that you're actually working on a machine that translates a dog's barks into words?"

"Yes. I've already recorded part of a sentence."

The room stopped. Sweet-Voice was holding it with one upraised hand as a deep, warbly, metallic voice sounded:

"I want to . . . ," then broke into shards of static.

She pulled me back in front of her face again, shook me, bit her bottom lip.

"I'm sorry, Angelly."

So many layers and tones it has, your world.

11

If there really were such a machine, and I had even a few barks left in me tonight, they would still be asking what is it you want, and how can I get it for you?

Deep sorrows, harbored grudges, regrets of the centuries? Your sphere, remember? I'm just the eager tagalong with the blunt view of pain.

Go, go, and further and on.

These things you feel you've lost—the purer beginnings, the wild origins that you keep looking for traces of in our eyes, and that you could, if you'd only come farther out into this darkness, hear strains of now in the cold, atom-stirring cries of the coyotes—all of these are in you still; all await you, still, around the next bend.

Follow me there. I'm hard on the path. Come away from your house's warmth to this dark wood's edge, and then, with me and the night sky, we'll begin to pour down, endlessly, through Dipper's bottomless cup.

Bugs. They're coming for me. Red ants, circling. Mosquitoes.

The flies will soon follow, and the crows, and the turkey buzzards. They'll all get whiff of this, come and turn me like a dying mouse.

If the coyotes don't come back first. I hear them now, far back in the forest, the faint yips, barks, and howls, spreading the news of me.

Why can't my masters hear it? Why can't they hear this night's wild ancestral cries and come running down to save me?

I'll have to do it all myself, have to drag myself the whole way back.

12

WHEN I'M BETTER. When I'm well again and back up there in the warmth of the cabin lights, and years of day-bones have passed, and someone really has built that machine, we should use it to straighten out all our head-tilts.

Like what it is you really want, and what are you so afraid of, and was there always a sphere of worry?

And how did your heads get to be so far from the ground, and your ears so odd looking, and your mouths so full of sounds?

And why do you leave us all the time, and where do you go, and why do you bring pine trees inside rooms?

It was a cold, clear day on Bosorne Road. The blue door opened and there was Huge-Head, carrying in a pine tree, bleeding that tingly-bitter-snow-fresh scent. He stood it in a corner in a dish of water, which muffled the trunk, but I could still hear the limbs ache and the slow wheeze of the needles.

Sweet-Voice brought out bags from the closet beneath the steep stairs, and together she and Huge-Head stood before the tree and began to dress it.

Head-tilt.

Strings of lights, brightly painted, spangelly bulbs, and long dangling trails of tinseled silver that raised my hackles just watching their ends drift and pat, like prehensile tails, the room's branching static.

They plugged in the tree. It looked like the one in the photo of Lucy that had fallen through the blue door a few days earlier: Lucy dressed in a set of bright red and white body-shadows and a pointed cap, its fluffy ball drooping alongside her snout.

They tried to put a paper hat on me that night. I scraped it off. Killed it. Everywhere flames sputtered atop pillars of white wax. Liquids of many colors—brown, gold, red—flowed, all combining to change the room, shepherd its wayward spirits, quiet all revolts. There was even, at long last, a series of fruitful hunts: the two of them burrowing into small, tightly wrapped boxes with things inside them, all useless to me, except for a box of biscuits.

They behaved that night as though there were far more of them in the room, and surely cooked that way, and later, after they'd spun in slow circles together through the warm-gravy air, and the candles had burned down, and the room filled up with the violent blue flashes, I got two big bellies to pad upon.

The following morning I was let out into the walled yard, then made my usual dash back inside, up the stairs, tuh-rump, tuh-rump, tuh-rump, tuuuuuh-rump, down into a stripped, icy-cold bed.

I hopped off, went to the door of Huge-Head's workroom. He was standing over an open case, folding body-shadows into it alongside pairs of feet-shadows, and stacks of books. I dashed back down the stairs. She was there, doing the same. Everything was going into cases and bags: bedding, books, dishes, bottles of the brown liquid. The tree? I watched from the front window as it was taken a short way down Bosorne Road and left beside the row of stinky bins.

The more their things were taken away, the sterner the room's air became. I grew edgy. Each time the blue door opened, I'd try to slip through it, but they were on to me. I ran back upstairs. There was an open case still on the bed. I shat in it. Huge-Head went crazy. Called me things, chased me back downstairs. I crawled behind the coal stove, cowered there for a while.

Why do these things happen?

Why would you suddenly abandon the very places you've so carefully adorned? Had we ferreted all the life from it, like a spent patch of forest that coyotes will desert in search of new prey?

I watched all the things I cared about—my bowl, my bag of food, my chew toys—get carried out. A last few cases followed. Soon there was just the furniture, and orphaned air, and the walled-in backyard of toppled plastic chairs and slow-turning goldfish. I hunched down between the cold front feet of the coal stove. Sweet-Voice went out. He followed. The blue door closed again.

Have you ever crept to the back of a just-closed door, pressed your nose to its base and sniffed, with all your heart, for some clue of when it might open again?

I got only the usual floor-dust and musty shoe-tread etched with shallow rivulets of salt sea air.

I heard footsteps. Two sets. Theirs. Getting neither louder nor more faint, going in brief, broken half-circles. A car door opened. Then another. One door closed. More footsteps. Just his, now, growing louder, coming toward me.

I backed away. The front door opened.

I don't think he'd ever seen me sit so politely before, a squat little spotted dollop of me set there on the carpet, looking up at him, my head slightly cocked, half out of its mind with urge and anticipation.

But I waited. I waited until he bent down for me and then sprung forward into his arms and clung to him while he fumbled about for the keys and locked the blue door for the very last time.

There was no room left for me in the car. I was to get her lap once again and those too-needy hands. I remember perching myself up against the dashboard, looking over the pasture walls at the cows grazing in the bright sunlight. Then the engine started and the world began to bob, and the sea to slowly recede.

Through an endless, sickening sky-swirl of winding hedgerows, the car, finally, came to the smooth, the straight way. There was only sun and clear sky when we left, but now the wind picked up and rain was falling.

"This damn country is God's weather workshop," Huge-Head muttered.

The rain fell harder. The car windows were pouring

within their frames. The two of them stopped talking. Her hands went different on me. Lost their give. Got a bit clammy.

"Maybe it's him," Huge-Head suddenly said, staring over at me.

Head-tilt.

"From the first night we got him he's been the conjurer of killer storms."

We do sense things, the about-to-happen, the disposition of every day toward dishevelment. You've heard, you know the stories, how we'll take off running in the moments before earthquakes, run sometimes until our paws bleed. How we'll go to the door and wait for you long before your actual return.

We're tuned to the things you can't hear, to extremes: your perfect constancy or its sudden absence; your undying devotion or your death. There's no middle ground for us, no half measure. Again, your province, the lukewarm, the static sphere of hope, and doubt and worry.

A woman drives her Boxer, Otis, two-beat tug, to the park for a run. They go there every afternoon, but this day Otis refuses to get out of the car. Won't budge. She finally gives up and drives home. The following afternoon, she returns to find a giant tree toppled across the exact spot where she'd parked the day before.

We're always trying to warn you about wayward atoms, even your own. There's a me, Jake, one-beat, from London. He was taken to a doctor because he wouldn't stop sniffing his master's leg. The doctor examined Jake and then his master's leg. The cancer was discovered just in time.

How many of you would still be counting day-bones if you'd listened? Roger, two-beats, a Labrador. He'd still have a home now if his owner hadn't ignored his warnings about the car she went to borrow from her neighbor. He tried to grab the keys from her hand, growled, bared his teeth, even chased after the car before finally falling away from it and the faulty steering atoms that would send his master hurtling into a stone wall and far along the path of souls.

Even as I sat there in her lap that day, in the driving rain, abiding her hands, I could feel the engine's ache, its dwindling will. We were headed up a long incline on the smooth way when the wiper arms began to slow in the thick water, and then the car came to a complete halt along the road's narrow shoulder.

"It's him," he said, again. "The little shit. Mayhem's personal messenger."

Her hands settled sweetly now around me.

"Shut up," she told him.

From one of the bags in the back, he grabbed a bright yellow body-shadow, put it on, stepped out. He went around to the front of the car, opened its hood, and looked in. Moments later he closed it again.

"Must be the goddamned alternator," he said, getting back behind the steering wheel. "I'll see if I can get someone to stop."

He got back out, stood at the front of the car in the gray torrents, waving his yellow arms. Cars, great lorries, thundered past, one after the next. She and I sat in the front seat, shivering, cold in our bones, unwarmable.

"Tummy, teat, and straw. Tummy, teat, and straw."

The car door opened. He said he was going down the embankment to try to stop a car on the smaller, country road that ran under the smooth way.

Right then I bolted. I don't know why. Every atom said to. Went straight over the embankment, riding the crest of her screams.

They both gave chase, following me down to the stone culvert running along the base of a tall wire fence that bordered a huge cow pasture. I went to where the fence met the country road, and then turned to watch the two of them coming toward me, yelling my name into the icy rain.

All at once, from high above us, there was a huge, screeching wail, like that of wild horses straining at new reins, followed by the crash of metal and the sight of the blue car flying forward, turning on its side in a spray of sparks, before rolling over completely and down the embankment, coming to rest on its head with a great crunch atop the culvert not twenty feet from where we stood.

Sweet-Voice began to cry. He held her. She reached down and picked me up.

"Angelly," she kept whispering, squeezing the life from me. "My smart little tough."

"Hello . . ." a faint voice sounded from above.

We could see through the rain just the shadowy outline of a man, waving. "Hello, is everyone all right?"

Soon we were all shivering together in the smash-faced cab of the man's lorry. More vehicles had arrived and everywhere there were lights swirling and blinking, blue and red and white. The blue car was eventually pulled up to the road's shoulder, bent and broken. All our things were pried out of the backseat and trunk and then the car was drawn away, through the walls of rain, never to be seen again.

That night I was confronted with yet another room to assess. It was one of many in a long, narrow hallway of rooms, and completely strange, with an ever-shifting unknowable scent, all on the surface, as though nothing in it really ever meant to be there.

When we did, at last, settle in that night, it was not like other nights, much warmer and closer and more desperate. I wedged myself into the mix. They both fell asleep before me, and I remember him now, his head resting right by mine, his lips pressed against both the pillow and the fur-tip of my right ear, saying, faintly, over and over to someone in a dream: "I'm sorry."

13

What do you dream about?

We dream of you and of food, about running after these, running so hard at times that our paws flip faintly beneath us back out in the waking world, and our barks bubble up there, too, in diminishing, puff-ball trails of "woofs."

We dream, in little snippets, of whatever places and things you've pulled our waking eyes past: cliffs, oceans, and farmland; of dark alleyways, soaring cities and the moons they strand.

I have dreamt of myself, quietly watching birds in trees, or snapping uncontrollably at the sunlight on a car fender. I've visited with my mother in dreams, lying in the cow-barn hay at Pollard's Combe. I've swum with those pond-blind goldfish. I even dreamt once of a steak. It was just lying there, alone on a sidewalk. I ate it.

Wild beasts often attack you in our dreams, as do the most beastly versions of you, the ones who kick us and poke our eyes out. We fend them all off. We guard your dreams as intently as we do the sphere of worry. No hierarchies of air. Every day is an open book of devotion to a me. That's why you keep us. I know that now.

You keep us because our devotion makes yours pale.

If there really is that machine, and I do climb this hill tonight, might it, softly, while I get some rest, translate for you all these sudden memories?

It was London that we nearly died trying to get to that cold rainy day, and London that I felt certain would kill me when we did.

Noise! As varied, as high and hard as its source, a whole other shadow-city of noise: foot-shuffle, horn-bleat and engine-grind; double-decker swine-snorts and two-tone siren blares—"Naaah—Naaah!" "Naaah—Naaah"—like crazed, unherdable sheep, everywhere laughing at me in a very bad dream.

The scents? I couldn't keep up. Would have drowned in them if Sweet-Voice hadn't been holding on to me: everywhere an air of expenditure and exhaust, of cooked essences, freshness stewed: coal, potato, fish, bread; twangs of spilled beer and briny fog; of offal and pot roast and old carpet; of paved rain and dead leaves.

Yes. That's it. London smells like a long-ago cemented autumn.

We made our way through the gnarled lanes of bulbous black cars, and I instinctually knew to narrow my focus, to just hunker down and hole up within one isolated smell, letting the rest of them fall away from me.

How long does it take to make so many rooms? Who thinks of them all, and who decides which one is yours, and how do you know how to find it?

I'd known some great cities before London. There was one at Pollard's Coombe, in the back corner of the cow barn, a towering carpenter ant's nest, taller than myself: populous rooms and passageways, urgent scamperings, endless appointments.

But it was made entirely of dust, spit, and straw. The merest brush of my snout would send sections tumbling. One day I inhaled a bit of straw and sneezed away whole neighborhoods.

My first close-up whiff of London was a high-rise at the corner of Gresse and Stephen streets. I bruised my snout badly. London has no give whatsoever.

Our little square of it was located near the bottom of a tall, brown stack of room squares, rising up from the dead end of Gresse Street in a section of town I think they call Soho.

Still, it was how they found our rooms that proved to be a great mystery to me. I was born to take the lead in hunts, but here I readily assumed my post at his sternum and watched.

Even when we arrived, we really hadn't yet. First, a glass door opened from the street, letting us into what seemed a very nice room as rooms go, but my masters seemed to know right off that it wasn't ours. This room gave way to a tiny one, not much bigger than a feed trough, the door to which slid open and closed by itself, and the whole of which—I know I didn't dream this— moved.

It must have moved because when the door opened again, a fly that had gotten in with us on the ground floor shot out and smashed straight into a wall that hadn't been there before. I could hear him, buzzing drunkenly on the floor as we walked away, still not in the right room. It was like we were peeling away the layers of the wild onions I used to dig up around Pollard's Combe, trying to get, at last, to the juicy core.

It was labeled Flat 2A, and looked and felt a lot like the room we'd just stayed in along the smooth way, the same shallow, shiftless scent, that restless air of imminent departure. There were two rooms actually, with bright blue carpets on the floor and loud, odorless paintings of flowers on the walls.

"Early Ramada," Sweet-Voice called it.

Head-tilt.

The flat wasn't very far in the end from the sliding feed trough. Its doors were forever rattling in my ears, haunting me during those long hours when the two of them would go out for the night, leaving me locked up alone within the padded crate. The one they'd bought especially for my long night's journey here to the new world inside the belly of the metal bird. The one they decided I should start getting used to early.

Nearly every night, it seemed, they'd change into a new set of body-shadows and then start moving rapidly back and forth between rooms in that way that all me's know means we're about to be left. I was always the last element of their departure ritual.

Sweet-Voice would be at the door—she wanted to remain on my good side—while he would swipe me up, place me inside the crate, toss in some toys and biscuits, secure the latch, and then start cooing good-byes in that high, fluttery tone that always left me feeling like the time I ate a whole stick of butter off the table in the Bosorne Road cottage.

As soon as they left, I'd set about the business of freeing myself, a little trick which Huge-Head to this day can't figure out how I managed. They'd come back through the door, reeking of smoke and brown liquid, to find me sitting there on the living-room sofa above gnawed chair-leg and feet-shadow pieces, and torn-up newspapers, wicker placemats and coasters.

"The little shit," he'd cry, going over to the crate, opening and closing the door, fiddling with the latch.

"He's goddamned Houdini!" Three-beat tug. Some dog I've never heard of.

Still, for all my efforts, I'd only freed myself into the larger prison of that flat, rooms I could never get to the bottom of, no matter how hard I dug.

There was a wide glass door at the back that opened onto a small stone balcony where a potted plant sat, dying. A few feet below it was a gravel rooftop with great metal mushrooms sticking up from it, spinning in place, as though trying to fly away. Behind them, more roofs tilted this way and that against the sky, where a giant tower rose so high that at night I could see the huge, metal birds slide, soundlessly, by, drawing the lit, upper-story windows with them into the outer darkness.

I'd wait. Chew. Wait. Listen.

Somehow, that room's quiet grew deeper, more deafening, within the widening expanse of the city's outer noise, each sound like another brick added to the walls of my aloneness: the crazed-sheep sirens, the exhaust snorts, the horse-whinny of lorry breaks—my former life at Pollard's Combe cemented now, mechanized.

I'd gnaw the couch leg, talk to myself. Machines are animals, too, Angus, just as sure as fish are metal: billions of supple, multi-shaped keys opening water's wide, ongoing lock.

I'd gnaw some more, stare off.

Fear.

But fear attached to no apparent danger or enemy. Sourceless dread. Is that what lurks in those invisible burrows of yours? Is that what stalks you in the sphere of worry?

Time passed. I'd begin to settle in, my lids to drift down, and then from the room directly above ours, the man, the unquiet man, would stir, talking, to no one, slurring his words into the night, as though angry at it, or frightened, like me, of the sourceless dread.

His voice would start to slide into eerie song. One day when Huge-Head was sitting out on the balcony, talking to me, the song spilled right down over us.

"I'm a Yankee Doodle Dandy . . ."

Head-tilt.

"I'm a Yankee Doodle cunt!"

Things got very quiet.

Huge-Head looked scared.

I hopped into his lap.

"It's okay, Angus," he said, his hand running along my back. "Just a nasty drunk."

Head-tilt.

I had big trouble with London. My daily walks? From hard balcony, to hard floor, to hard lobby, to hard sidewalk, to hard street, and everywhere only broken gray shards of visible sky above. In the end, the outdoors seemed to me not very different than the in, so I often shat and pissed in.

Huge-Head would grab the leash from the closet, drag me into the feed trough and out through the front door to the sidewalk, where he'd promptly place me, like a wind-up toy, down.

"Outside!" he'd shout. "Outside!"

Head-tilt.

He'd start away.

Paw-burn.

I didn't want to lead. I wanted to go back in. I'd already checked up and down Gresse Street. The only available earth was at the base of a couple of sycamores, both of them trapped inside iron railings.

Trees in rooms? Trees behind bars?

They're not a threat to run, you know, trees. They're very good that way. Stolid, mute witnesses. They hid the coyotes tonight until the very last second, then just stood by as I was brought down among them.

Huge-Head and I did eventually work out a compromise that allowed us to get around London together. When we were headed away from the flat, I was to be carried. When we started home, I took the lead, full bore.

We'd go out in the morning for the paper and the coffee and the bread and the brown liquid, and everywhere the hands and high, fluttering voices—with many new, strange tones to them now—would rain down upon me.

But I never dozed up there at his sternum, taking in every step of the journey out so that the moment I felt him starting back toward Gresse, I'd fuss to get down and then start pulling toward home like a plow horse.

There was a pub nestled into one corner of Gresse

where it bends toward Rathbone Street. Huge-Head always tried to steer past it so that the young ladies sitting at the sidewalk tables could lay the snare of their needy little hands all over me and—if there is such a thing as touching with your eyes—he his all over them. I'd suffer this ordeal on the way out, but coming back, I'd pull to the far side of the street, and Huge-Head—not wanting to be seen inflicting paw-burn on an innocent puppy—always obeyed.

In this way, in these testy little increments, I came to know London, to learn things.

I learned that while you do scurry along like ants—heads down, briefly bumping into one another, brushing antennae, getting the message, continuing on—you also eddy and pool a lot, in pointless pockets, on park benches and in cafés, only to stare back out at all the scurrying.

How is it that you can have a mission and open permission to deny it?

So many layers and tones.

It wasn't long before I was taking the lead in London, our walks there, I realized, being merely upside-down versions of the ones in Cornwall: Huge-Head, Sweet-Voice, and me, moving along the base of cliffs rather than the top of them. Most days, we'd walk to a part of town they called Bloomsbury. We'd go to the same park, Russell Square: small stands of jailed trees with people sitting on benches, or strolling along, many of them with their me's. At night, the place looked entirely different: benches empty, furtive men in long, dark body-shadows, hunched up against the base of trees, like huge hanging bats.

Me's, I saw them everywhere. Where do so many get made? Dogs of every size and shape, hurrying along or waiting with you. Going in and out of doors, or sitting up at the windows of even the highest room-stacks, checking for the earth, watching out for more dogs moving past, the owned and the disowned.

Every night in the London rooms, I'd feel them out there, the strays, roaming, namelessly, a shadow city of hard scents, their trails twisting and crossing in pliant, supple threads, their barks and howls as clear to me still as those of the coyotes here tonight.

Did you know, have I told you, that city me's often abandon you out of boredom, get so crazed in your closed rooms that they run the first chance they get and wander your streets without you?

They don't form true packs again, like those of the coyote and the wolf and the wild dog, don't ever retrieve that part of themselves. Whether they roam alone or together, they remain rogues at heart, like you, separate, lone travelers, broken-off pieces of the younger world, going forward, through the light and dark halves of each day, one after the next, like you.

I had a dream in London, a strange dream. I remember it now. I was alone in our flat, my cage door open, me lying on the sofa, staring out the back glass doors at the metal birds sliding through the upper lit windows of the tall tower, the unquiet man strangely quiet, my lids going heavy.

I dreamt about a far more distant future than the next fallen tree or crashed car or case of cancer.

I dreamt that you, that all of you, deep down inside, want to leave us dogs, leave us and the ground that we still like to dig in, behind; that you want to escape your very own bodies, leave them and all the ways that they fail you, behind.

This, I suddenly sensed, is what you've been after all along, what you've been digging for in those unseen burrows in the airy, the groundless part of each day, digging past even that idle, sourceless dread in hopes of finding it.

You leave us. You go through some immeasurably vast door, and close it on us, the ones who've come so far with you; who've been pulled by you so far from our

original purpose that we've become by now the house-
bound, shedding vestiges of a time that was once all
time; yapping vessels of dead-end behaviors: burying
chew-bones that we never mean to dig up again; humping couch pillows in your skyborne rooms; chasing our
tails just so the world will keep moving when we stop;
chewing your foot-shadows and then blithely present-
ing them when you come through the door, just to feel
the echo weight in our jaws of bearing home to a pack
leader some hard-won prey.

There is a terrier, two-beat tug, Franky.

He took every biscuit ever given him by his master
and buried each one, leaving their tops sticking above
the grass, filling an entire backyard with them until it
looked like a field of weathered tombstones.

Another terrier, Staffordshire, pit bull, female, one-
beat tug, Eve?

She was cast out on the streets by her owner after
giving birth to a litter of eight. All of them were taken
away at four weeks to be trained in back rooms for the
fighting you're too cowardly to do with each other.

Eve was found, alone, roaming the streets of her
own namelessness. She was eventually taken in again,
but could never truly recover, could never get to the
bottom either of her new comfort or her old pain. Just

to sleep at night, she'd have to gather up her chew toys and arrange eight of them in a tight semicircle about her belly.

Haven't we, then, minds and hearts like yours?

And still, in my dream, you leave us. The door closes, and we, all of the world's me's, are left waiting on the other side, sniffing the bottom edge of the jamb, the thin crack of light, for some suggestion of where you've gone, and of when you might return.

But there's nothing. Not a rush of wind. Not a scent. No one to greet us again or to be greeted by us. No one to come back and call out the one-, two-, or however-many-beat tugs that pull us into brief, tail-wagging frenzies of self-recognition and joy. All the world a scentless, vacated hallway of withering, uncalled me's.

I barked so long and hard in my sleep that night, I awoke to find that the wind of my waking-world woofs had made a perfect halo of torn wicker coaster bits around my head. I have no real sense of time, but the rest of that night seemed to drag on well toward forever until, at last, the front door opened again.

They came home.

You do, finally, all come home.

That's how my dream ends. You don't ever get away, from yourselves or us; don't find a damn thing in those groundless burrows. You come home, sit down, have another sip of the brown liquid, and hold on to us well into the small hours; you's and me's, side by side, in an ever-widening world of stacked rooms and worry. We sit and wait and watch, going over to the window, now and again, putting our hands and paws on the sill, looking out over the prickly grid of lights to check for the earth again, and the other you's and me's, and the metal birds drifting past.

"What's he thinking?" Huge-Head always asks when he sees me looking out the window.

She never answers him. I feel she knows. She's just too impatient to hunt for the words.

14

"An—gus?"

Think, Angus.

Where am I?

Peepers. Stars. Darkness. Earth. Sweet field grass beneath me. Cool tickle of wind now across my punctured, saliva-soaked back.

I'm so hurt.

Memory.

Can I remember my way home? Not the way home. Can I be conveyed by memories, home? Do memories ever get you anywhere?

I remember leaving London.

Nighttime in a port of air, staring out through the bars of my padded crate as it was being conveyed away from the earth toward the round, glossy belly of the metal bird.

I remember having, as usual, no idea what was happening to me.

I remember now that you leave places without warning; that there seems to be for you, as there is with the air inside rooms, a hierarchy of rooms; that you live in some with more desire and determination than you do others.

Those along the smooth way you inhabit and discard like the bones we bury and never retrieve. Others, like our London flat, are dwelled in, turned over and returned to enough times to make any me believe that they are, for you, the most delicious and worthy and lasting of rooms, only to discover that you have a whole other set of rooms to which only remnants of the previous ones and all the things that occurred in them are brought, things to be stored in boxes or left lying around for an occasional listless lick like so many discarded me-toys.

We will remain forever in the dark, won't we, about your moves, about what moves you?

I remember the night before we left our London rooms, the night of the unquiet man. Was he the one who made us leave? Day after day we'd hear his singing and carrying on. And then one day, nothing, not a peep. And nothing further for days after that.

"Perhaps he's moved," Sweet-Voice said, sitting on the living-room sofa one evening, those needy hands pulling my ear flaps taut above my head, then releasing them, soothing, in a way that I'm sure she sensed, the deep itches that lurk within every me's brain.

"Good riddance," said Huge-Head.

But soon afterward I began to sense a change in our flat. A damp, gathering vacancy that seemed to emanate from the area of the front hallway.

Hallways are fairly straightforward landscapes, a set of wall and ceiling atoms. These were a bit different from others I'd seen before, surface expanses of tiny white waves, stuck, mid-swell, but they always seemed to be staying the course, holding their own.

The first few times I went out and checked, I saw nothing. Then I noticed a slight buckling of paint where the ceiling's waves met the wall's between the front door and the bath. I decided to keep an eye on it, made a point of going, throughout the day, to that end of the hallway, and sitting and staring up at the tiny warp in the whiteness, sitting and staring and sniffing and listening.

Had there been drops of water falling somewhere

behind the walls, I'd have heard them and sized up the situation sooner. But this turned out to be the much sneakier sound of water trying to be a wall—a thin sheet of it cascading down along the wall's back side until it reached to the bottom and then started being a floor. I craned my neck way back. In the ceiling's glass light fixture, a little pool was gathering.

As the hours passed, the wall-warp grew, a slow-burgeoning buckle, as if the entire hallway was infinitesimally doubling, then tripling itself.

I was too intrigued to bark or make a fuss. This was the first exciting thing to happen in that place, especially later that evening, when Huge-Head went to the front closet to get their coats for yet another night out. He flipped on the hallway's overhead light.

Pow!

I love it when atoms do finally revolt.

"What the hell was that?" said Sweet-Voice, coming into the hallway. She stopped. I watched her eyes rove up and over and around the walls.

"I'd get up there right now," she said, "and tell that asshole he's left his tap on."

I ran to the front door to go with him. It slammed in my face.

I waited for the clanking of the feed-trough. Instead the stairwell door just opposite ours squeaked open, the rush of air briefly flipping up our mail slat, tickling the tip of my nose.

Head-tilt.

Footsteps scraping skyward, like the pinging sound of little stones dropped down a well.

Door squeak.

A few more steps.

He was directly above us now.

Two knocks, tentative, not nearly loud enough. He was nervous.

Long pause.

Sweet-Voice began sweeping up the shards of broken lightbulb. I grew frantic. She came over, picked me up. Those hands.

"It's okay, Angus."

More knocks, louder now.

Long pause.

A door opening. The stairwell door again. I knew the squeak.

Footsteps descending.

"No one home," Huge-Head said, coming back inside.

I sniffed it on him instantly, unmistakable, emanating from his lower pant legs. Death! Old death! Too far gone even for my liking. That rotten-egg, mildewed-brussel-sprout, sweet-tanged, wet-leather molder of at least the third—judging from my old, ripening Pollard's Combe carcasses—and perhaps even the fourth day after the departure of the force that animates all atoms.

They had no idea, my masters, kept feeling the hallway, talking about how hot the walls were getting around the light switches. They then put a pail beneath the exposed ceiling fixture and prepared to leave.

Huge-Head placed me in my crate. Before heading out the door, he went to the closet, opened a small metal box on the back wall, and flipped off a row of thick switches that made all the lights in the flat go out and the air collapse. I heard the front door close, the feed trough clank open and shut, and there I was, alone in the darkness beneath a slow-trickling waterfall of death.

The whole night, I never left the crate. Just lay there on my white pad, trembling, listening to the hallway widen, trying to find one sweet spot for my nose amidst the creeping tendrils of body rot.

Blink . . . and . . . blink.

No sleep. No dreams. Just my breathing, and the flat, and those back glass doors, and London's off-kilter roofs, and the metal birds, sliding past the tall tower, pulling still more windows into the outer dark.

Was his the room that the unquiet man wanted to be in when he left for the path of souls? Or did he have, as we did, still others that he was about to fly away to the very next day, some other home that he may have been longing to get to?

Longings? I know them. Can you get home on the back of them, those little ghost rabbits that suddenly crop up in my brain and get me nowhere, send me in senseless, tail-chasing circles?

Think, Angus.

You are nothing now if not a longing, one deep longing, inch by inch, without a second, not even a first thought; an urge, an instinct, trying to climb away from the consequences of responding to your last one.

15

"An—gus?" "An-gus!"

Her. Sweet-Voice, right there, outlined in the glow of the cabin lights.

Where is that conveyor belt now?

I remember—what good is it?—I remember sliding upward toward the belly of the metal bird, wide-eyed and clueless through a deafening high-pitched whine of fumes, seeing out my crate's side slats the world's largest beak, shiny and unbreathing. Then I passed into the shadowy hold.

A pair of hands set me down.

More animal crates, large and small, arrived, all around me against the hold's pale light: a smelly mini-skyline of creatures in a room about to enter the sky.

Who thought of that?!

The lights went down. A door—whumph!—closed.

Tummy, teat, and straw. Tummy, teat, and straw.

We started to roll. Barking. Couldn't see where it was coming from. I kept gnawing at the crate door. Huge-Head had it wired on all sides. Next to me, a gray parrot, wide-eyed, perfectly still, watched. Beside him, the pair of emu, huge, flightless things, walking haystacks with the pitchfork still sticking out the top.

Across the way, three heavily drugged horse heads drooped over the bars of their narrow travel stalls, the lips of the horse on the far right gently bobbing against the bald head of a man asleep on a little fold-out stool. A leather case at his hip held a huge syringe and a bottle of clear fluid.

The rhinoceros was off to my far left, asleep on his feet, his breathing heavy and broken, like a stalling tractor motor, his horn, swaying, ever so slightly, from side to side, hypnotizing the entire hold.

We stopped rolling, the force pulling the horse's lips smack down on the sleeping man's head. He woke without moving a muscle, his eyes looking right at me, like a suddenly animate doll.

"Hallo, little one," he said. "What's your name, eh?"

He stood, came toward me, wiggled a finger in through my crate's door slats.

I bit it.

"Bugguh! Little shite! Try that again and you'll get some of this tranquilizer I've been saving for my friend here."

Head-tilt.

We started rolling again, a steady, rapidly building rumble, the engines whining to the top of night's ceiling, and then the earth just dropping out from under us. I bit down on my heart. The rhino threw out a searching front foot, nearly busting through the floor. The parrot bumped its head on the top of his cage.

"Ahhp. Flying now! Flying now."

"Shut up, yah silly bird!" The man sat back on his fold-down stool, pulled a bottle of the brown liquid from his breast pocket.

"A lot of shite for a free plane ticket, eh, my simple friends?"

The water in my crate's drink bottle was tilted at a severe angle. Slowly, it flattened out again. Stayed that way for a long time. Footsteps knocked against the floor above, all along the belly of the bird's constant going. I felt like an about-to-be-swallowed meal, like the ant I once saw at the Combe, clinging to a shard of wood adrift in the cow's water trough.

I remember now, not very far into my life, wandering off behind the barn at the Combe. I went down a hole. A rabbit hole. It led to another one and then another, tunnels going in all directions, a downward-branching tree of air. Urges drew me farther down, from tunnel to tunnel, the narrower the passage the better, all leading nowhere but into themselves. My heart began to hurry, and my breath to chase after it, too far along either to turn back or to see a way out.

I sat there in my cage far above the earth, in the belly of the metal bird, endlessly boring through its skyward tunnel, and, just as I did that day in the hole beneath the Combe, began to bark.

"What's eatin you, yah little bugguh?"

Worm by worm, mite by mite, I began making my way back out of that rabbit hole. Tummy, teat, and straw . . . Tummy! Teat! Straw! and there, suddenly, was my mother, grabbing me by the extra skin, pulling me out and back to the barn, its haystrewn floor as clear and fine in my mind now as the ground that finally reached up that night and, with a great screech, grabbed the metal bird.

"So long, little bugguh!"

The hold door swooshed open on a new port of air. Crate by crate, I watched the creature city get dismantled, lowered to the earth: the rhino, still sleeping, the emu, the horses, the parrot. Then me. Right behind me a large wooden pallet of alpaca descended, heads aswivel.

I sat there on the runway beside a cart piled high with crates and bags. No one would lift mine onto it. All around me, bone-blue lights and the roar of landings and leavings, and high up against the night sky, a round glass nest with the shadow of a man inside, watching over everything.

I looked back up at the metal bird, lights bleeding over its shiny skin, a row of heads filing past tiny round windows. At one, I could see the outline of Sweet-Voice. She was banging, noiselessly, at the glass, waving down to me, mouthing my name, over and over, like a little pond-blind goldfish.

An—gus! An—gus!

I'm coming.

I do mean to come now.

16

LUCY.

I can still smell Lucy. Can still feel her out there tonight somewhere along the path of souls.

Would I be in this condition now if she were around, if she hadn't left me alone here just weeks after we arrived?

All these questions, Angus. Where are they getting you?

"An-gus?" "An—gus!"

Why can't they see me?

Am I still here? I can't even feel my body anymore. How strange that I, Angus, would amount to little more than the sum of my thoughts—a faintly firing atom-snare atop a numbed carcass of atoms.

Where am I exactly?

Dipper. Ground, treeless. Cabin lights. Sealed buttercups and Indian paintbrush hovering all around me. Smell them, Angus. It's the north field, not too far from where Sweet-Voice likes to sit in the afternoon under the tattered orange beach umbrella that she sets on its side and rolls in hourly increments through the grass—a felled sun eclipsing the light of the real one.

I can't be far off now.

Over there is the gnarled, low-slung arm of the old crab apple tree. There the hedge of wild roses where I'm always losing things. Farther on, I can see the early moonlight firing the leaves of the silver birch that Lucy liked to lay beneath.

Lucy.

She wouldn't have been much help tonight. Not just because she couldn't stand me. I understood that from the first moment we bumped noses. It was the day after we landed on this side of the world, and I was introduced to the flat in Brooklyn, to "home."

It looked like just more rooms to me, a lot more—a kitchen, a living-, a dining-, a bath-, and two bedrooms—all with the same scheming furniture and orphaned air. First thing I did when the front door opened was run to the window to check for the earth. It was a long way down and cemented for as far as I could see: endless, terraced pastures of black with the tops of trees rearing up here and there in between them like the riled manes of furrow-bent plow horses.

Head-tilt.

It was much like the view from the hill above Pollard's Combe but with less bend, less sway in it.

Brooklyn smelled different from London. Brooklyn smelled like a newly paved pasture; like a sunlit, just-slept-in bed; like the wide sea barely held at bay in the wings of one drifting, inland gull.

I could hear me's everywhere, strained-leash barks echoing up against the sides of buildings. But I saw only one, a very thin one nestled beside a scraggly man sitting on a sofa that's set out on the sidewalk alongside his other furniture and his bags of body-shadows. A room in which the orphaned air is all of air.

Head-tilt.

I could smell and see Lucy everywhere in the Brooklyn rooms, Lucy captured over and over again in the motionless days. In one she looks to be even younger than I was when I was first taken from the Combe: a little cup of spots in the side pocket of Sweet-Voice's coat. In another she's just about my age now, she and Huge-Head lying intertwined on a couch, sound asleep.

She's up here at the cabin in most of the others: Lucy splashing through the reeds of the back pond; sunning herself atop a rotting picnic table here in the north field; blending into the mottled sunlight beneath the silver birch, the spot I could never get her to budge from during our brief time here together.

The morning after we landed on this side of the world, we got in a car and drove—I don't know where or for how long—to get Lucy from the the letter-writing ladies. I know we left Brooklyn, left the city. More sky was arriving in my eyes. On and on, and drone and blab, and blurred trees, and nausea and on, and then the car stopped in front of a small white house trapped inside a lawn.

We walked up to a side door. Knocked. Sweet-Voice held me in her arms. The door opened. A dense, acrid wave of creaturely odors washed over me: dog, cat, fish, bird. I struggled to free myself, to find a more base, a common scent around which to order all the others. We were in a kitchen of screaming light and fake animals on the walls made of wood and plastic with smiley faces and flowers on them.

Everyone was talking too loud, mostly the ladies— big, round sisters. They looked exactly alike. They kept pointing to a row of foul-smelling little brown bottles with white caps, some with black rubber teat-shaped tops.

"This is for her failing kidneys."

Head-tilt.

"This is for her leaky-bladder problem. Her hips are arthritic, but this helps her get around, and we've been applying this to her skin blisters."

We started down a narrow hall off the kitchen. The air got closer, hopelessly clogged with scent. A door opened. A parrot and a canary fluttered up against their cages, feathers flying. Tropical fish—luminous, finned lozenges—drifted through a wall-length, lighted tank. Cats swirled about the furniture. From one sofa, two dogs rose, came toward us for a sniff.

I kept scanning the room, trying to locate the rusty-dander, stale-biscuit essence. Then, from a side sofa, came a steady stream of delayed, muffled woofs: Lucy, trying to focus through a pair of red, milky eyes.

She'd gotten her two front paws to the floor, but was struggling to bring the back half of herself along so she could help protect her new home against these intruders, who, as she finally got herself fully down and then wobbled into the limbo of midroom, she suddenly recognized as her entire life.

She wiggled once, the whole of her, as though trying to slough off, in one motion, her age. And then she started crying and wiggling, too fast, in all directions and from within, getting more and more cries out, faster and faster, that they might begin to catch up with and somehow equal her sadness and her joy.

Huge-Head bent down on one knee, grabbed hold of her. She worked her way free, wiggled around some more, came back to him.

Sweet-Voice began to cry, placed me down on the floor. Lucy went to her, burrowing farther and farther into Sweet-Voice's embrace until her spotted head popped out the back, where I was waiting, nose first, to greet her.

She bit me.

A little nip, but it set the tone.

Things never advanced much beyond that between us. Anyone could see that Lucy was near the end of her days, and that I was the last thing she needed: a bundle of puppy vigor, a two-bit, tricolored taunt. She hated me right down to the fresher smell of my young atoms.

In the days that followed, we fought over everything, from the sunlight squares that pooled each afternoon on the Brooklyn dining-room floor, to that prime pocket of warmth in bed at night between Sweet-Voice and Huge-Head.

Lucy was the runt of her litter. I recognized that right off. Runts arrive wild-eyed and jumpy into this world, and never quite feel at home in it. It's in their atoms. They chase their tails a lot, and need to maul anything you try to cushion a day with: sofas, pillows, mattresses.

Upholstery is no buffer for a runt against things like a sudden clap of thunder. One stormy night a few months ago after Huge-Head and Sweet-Voice had gone out, I watched Lucy make quick work of the living-room sofa, digging down through the cushions, stuffing flying everywhere.

I was always trying to prod her into play, but she'd fend me off with a furious flurry of snarls, wanting no part of my efforts to break the boredom of those Brooklyn apartment days: the hours of going to the windows to make the occasional earth-checks; and waiting for the sunlight squares to appear on the dining-room floor; and going back and forth between our meals and the sofa, or the sofa and the bed.

A little game I invented with a rubber ball and the living-room coffee table galled Lucy the most. Perhaps because in all of her years there she never came up with it herself: put the ball on the lower support rung of the table, hold it there with your front paw for a moment, then let go and watch the ball fall to the floor.

I'd play it for hours, each fascinating plop and furry dribble of the ball across the floor driving Lucy over the edge, the arthritic back half of her lurching along the sofa as she snarled and snapped at my haunches.

I liked Lucy, guarded her with my life. Ruined by age and the double-edged pain of having been deserted so late in life only to be greeted again by the likes of me, she'd already begun to withdraw from this world, and I felt the least I could do was try to protect her from it on all flanks as she did.

We'd go each day for our afternoon walks in a big swath of cement-bound trees called Prospect Park.

Odd place.

Just enough trees and sky to make you think you've left the city, and yet from everywhere still come the hard scents and sounds of it, everywhere the sphere of worry wilting the edges of the trees.

Out across the park's long meadow, strands of scampering me's would weave in and around static semicircles of you's, standing there, making even the outdoors feel like another closed room, talking on and on about us, our habits, our misdeeds, and all kinds of nonsense about what we think and want and why it is that one of us is humping the other's head while a third latches on from behind, and then a fourth in a jerky, ever-reassembling, multiheaded mutt of unleashed urge.

"He's the alpha!"

"She's definitely the dominant female."

"That's classic pack behavior manifesting as . . ."

Shut up!!!!!!

That's all over! We're with you now, remember; are just like you now: lonely vessels of dead-end behavior, humpers of couch pillows in skyborne rooms, confused rogues.

We'd enter the park. Lucy would show an initial burst of excitement, then pull up in pain, spending the rest of the time sitting there in the grass at Huge-Head and Sweet-Voice's feet, spinning cockeyed circles on her arthritic hips to get to her own asshole.

If another me approached, Lucy would fly off into her snaps and snarls, and I'd pounce. It made no difference what it was. The most bulked-up pit bulls and rottweilers, Akitas and shepherds have all felt the full weight of my terrier tenacity. Ask the Prospect Park dogs, if you do ever get that machine worked out. Ask them about the crazed Jack Russell from Devon who backs down from no one, who bites down and can't be shaken off.

"An—gus?"

Yes. Keep calling. Keep the moving world at bay.

She'd have been no good to me tonight, Lucy, even if she had lived. Even if she were still young and healthy, she wouldn't have made any difference. There are me's who go forward into danger and those who are frozen by it, who retreat even as they bare their fangs and growl. They can't help it. It's something inside them, a built-in hopelessness, something I've never known.

Nothing gives me pause. It got so they couldn't even let me off the lead anymore in the Brooklyn park. They'd have to walk me across the long meadow and let me run in a section of forest that was fenced off for repairs.

Head-tilt.

How does a forest get broken?

Huge-Head, Sweet-Voice, and Lucy would stand on the far side of a NO TRESPASSING sign while I slipped under the gate and disappeared among the trees. Thousands of them. A wood much like the one here behind me tonight, except that most of the fear had been removed from it, the thrill that comes with the chance that you won't come back out of it alive—that heightened, tensile, hackle-dance thrill of the younger, the moving world.

I'd make them wait by that fence well past dark . . .
"An—gus?" "An-gus!". . . echoing among the trees as I
chased all the squirrels up them, and the rats down into
their holes, and the birds wherever the hell it is they go.
Little old me putting a charge into the place, stirring
things up, testing the limits of my new life before having to return home to its slow, familiar, bittersweet core:
light cream with a trace of wheat and wild onion; distant
barley-bear-musk; old miss dying-dog-dander-rust; and
me, what did I smell like then, like freshly cut, sun-
warmed hay; the four of us, sitting around in the Brooklyn rooms, staring at each other, checking out the
windows for the earth and the other me's.

They have no idea of this, but one day in the depths
of the fenced-off woods, I found myself running with a
bunch of strays who'd found shelter in an abandoned
brick guardhouse at the top of the glacial ridge that cuts
through the broken Brooklyn forest. The thing about
strays is they don't mind you a bit, couldn't care less.
They go about their days in a stealthy, knit-brow self-
absorption that you can either meld or depart with, but
never make add up to anything more than the sum of
separates, searching.

I couldn't sleep that night, thinking about the strays.
My heart kept going away from me. I got up, walked

about the Brooklyn rooms. Lucy got up, too, dragged her painful hips out of bed and stood there in the hallway—Lucy drowsily watching over me now as I wandered the apartment like a little ghost, passing under the dining-room table, feeling the brush of tablecloth along my back, and then again as I emerged out the far side, into the looming otherness of rooms.

I stood staring, blankly, at the wall of motionless days. Went over to the windows, listened to the city pulsating like a huge cricket in a corner of night.

Many nights since, I've run with those strays, have fallen off into dreams and then pawed the air in pursuit of the nameless me's.

"An—gus!"

Listen.

She knows something's wrong. I can hear it in her voice. She'll run inside and tell him now, tell him that tonight is different, that I really am in trouble this time, that she can feel it.

She knew all along that there would be something different about tonight. She'll remember, later, after I'm back there with them in the cabin lights, remember the way I tried to let her know, just this afternoon as she sat here in the north field.

She seems so close to me now.

I can't have much farther to climb.

Unless I haven't been climbing at all.

Unless I've been dreaming all of this as well, and am still lying back down there at the wood's edge, doing the phantom woofs and paw swipes now as the coyotes gather around me, watching, licking my blood, waiting for the twitching to stop, nuzzling one of the young pups forward to finish me off so that it can bear home the prey, the dumb Jack Russell, the hard-bitten soul, indeed.

17

ROLL . . . PLOP . . . DRIBBLE . . . SNARL . . .

Roll . . . plop . . . dribble . . . snarl . . . the safe, the
sweetly boring string of Brooklyn day-bones that could,
for all I knew, have added up to my entire life, and then,
suddenly, this. A chance to die like this.

If I don't make it back tonight. If I'm gone by the
time you find me here in the north field, gone to meet
Lucy and all the other me's already out there along the
path of souls, you will know, won't you, how good it was
for me to have been brought here and given a chance to
die like this?

No regrets. No blame. Thrust of chance. They were
getting too close, and I charged, headlong, into more

than I knew, into a part of myself far greater than I ever knew.

Have you felt this?

Have you ever felt what I do now: a complete awareness of the depth of my own recklessness and yet not one regret? As hard and long as I might climb to get back to you tonight, I can't ever make my way far enough into the sphere of worry to know real regret. Can't ever make myself think that I've ruined things for you, that I've wrecked your hopes, broken your hearts. I can't make myself think anything except that if I were able to feel something now, I'm certain that this thinking would hurt.

Is it enough that we couldn't care less for your plans or regrets, and yet any more deeply for you and for the moment at hand? I've never wanted one thing—not a mouse, not a badger, not a sidewalk dream-steak— more than I want to get back now to you within the warm fold of the cabin lights and the woodstove fire and the suggestion—however faint it might be for a me— that there will be another day on the far side of this one through which to charge headlong again and recklessly.

What are you up there thinking now?

What are any of you out there thinking?

Head-tilt . . . head-tilt.

So many-sided, your brains. I couldn't have made the charge into these woods tonight with one. Or this long climb back now.

We proceed one thought at a time, and even then we can be so easily put off it. You've seen us, the way we'll get stuck, midthought, in your rooms, heads drooping, trying to recall what it was we were on our way to do.

Peepers.

I hear them still, from the back pond, but so faintly now. I'm either nearer to home or to the path of souls, the only difference between those anymore being them, my masters, the chance at another moment with them.

She's stepping back into the cabin.

Tell him.

Tell him something's wrong, that something's happened.

Quickly. They'll be coming back to finish me soon.

How did this happen, Angus?

So quickly. One minute I'm bearing down, closing in on the scent, like nothing I've known—raw, deeply primordial me—and the next: scissor-flash, and star-swirl, and my body going hard against the earth.

Where did they come from? I had this entire place under control. These fields are crisscrossed with the matted-down trails of my daily, frenzied charges away from the cabin into the outer woods, keeping all the threats at bay.

"Dog heaven."

You would say that of here, of where I am dying. Huge-Head always calls it "dog heaven."

It is, but not in the way you think. It's not as though we bask like you in the open views, in the dizzying and, for us, extra deep array of scents. The place is nonstop work to keep track of and to guard, and work is what pleases us most.

So much of it here for one me. I started the moment we arrived, at night, the car turning onto ever smaller roads, into ever darker skies, fewer lights than even at the Combe. We steered up a steep hillside of woods, the headlight beams thwacking the tree trunks, Lucy whining with each turn, me with my paws up on the dashboard, head snapping, nose twitching off the scents.

Here the base-note scent is, I don't know, of the younger world and timeless; of fungus, fern, lichen, and moss; of quartz-moist and drifting spore. Here the atoms don't argue as feverishly with their present frames because so few of those have been shaped by you: only the car, ticking and pinging all day under its own weight in the field grass at the top of the entrance road; and the cabin itself—an old, rotting square of trees half-swallowed now by the very forest they came from.

All this untamed openness. It was disorienting at first. I had no idea what my job was. I did discover the pieces of a working farm here, the rusted tips of plows, feed troughs, and horseshoes, protruding here and there from the field grass: all the irretrievably buried bones of my old life at the Combe.

Huge-Head and Sweet-Voice certainly offered me no hints about how to be. They'd driven us all those hours into this complete absence of cement and lights only to do here exactly what they do back in the city: sit around and stare off into the unseen burrows. Who are they, I often wonder as I sit, staring at them, these masters who the thrust of chance has bound my devotion to? Are the rest of you like them: ghosts of utility, tillers of the air?

As for Lucy, she was just too old, too diminished by her own inability to answer the constant call of this place. She'd hole herself up all day on the bed beneath the cabin woodstove, or, when the sun got high and hot enough, in the mottled light beneath the silver birch.

Within a few weeks her life here had dwindled down to one or two pained waddles between the woodstove and her water bowl. On the sunny days, Huge-Head would have to carry her out to her spot beneath the silver birch, where her dwindled frame seemed to fade in and out of the spotted light. At night, she had to be carried up to the loft bed so she could sleep with us.

I'd stop by to see her in the course of my daily forays, ever-edgey, runt-mad Lucy, so jealous of my youth's unbridled freedom and all the delicious scents I always came back to the cabin wearing, that she'd immediately send me away on the vibratory crest of her snaps and snarls.

She wasn't attacking me so much as she was the approach of her own life's end, trying to fend it off and then collapsing from the effort, into the grass, licking at all her body's leaks before finally settling in again with a shimmery sigh to watch these fields of her best days fall forever away from her.

And then, one day, from the deep woods, I heard the sound of the car starting. They always start the car here as a last-ditch gesture to get me back. It never fails. I do, after all, know who feeds me. The two of them were already sitting up in the front seat when I returned. Lucy was in the far back, head drooped, staring out the window at me with those sunken, asking eyes. She had the most asking eyes.

"Get in the car, Angus," Sweet-Voice said in that icy tone her voice gets when she means business. "Now!"

We wound our way down the mountain to where the road smooths, and then the world was going by very fast and Sweet-Voice's hands all up and down me.

We had to stop at the crest of a long, narrow road through a tall field of corn, the sun glaring off the waxen stalks. Just ahead, plumes of acrid-rubber smoke were billowing up around a fast-spinning car set high above its back wheels, like a scared cat on its haunches.

Head-tilt.

We watched it go round and round and then pull off into the shadows of a roadside barn, the car's fat, bare-armed driver staring back at us as we disappeared into his stinky wake.

On the far side of the cornfield we came to a white house inside a lawn with a tall white sign on it. Huge-Head went around to the back of the car. He picked up Lucy, bed and all, and walked her in through a side door, Sweet-Voice following closely behind, a waft of something chemical, biting, trailing past my slightly opened car window. I perched up against it, stared out, and watched for that side door to open again.

Off behind the white house, there was a gently sloping field of tombstones, like a stunted city. A car was winding its way among them. It stopped. People got out. They stood there above one of the stones, heads drooped. Someone stepped forward, placed a bunch of flowers on the ground.

Head-tilt.

The side door opened again. Sweet-Voice. She didn't come over to me. Just stood there in the lot, looking up into the air. Where is everyone always looking? She took a deep breath, then went back inside.

Some time later, the door opened again. Huge-Head. He stood around, too, doing nothing, breathing kind of strangely before he turned and went back inside.

We won't ever be able to talk to each other, will we?

Perhaps in a million day-beads. Centuries of you talking to us in your skyborne rooms, far away from all our other purposes except the one of being devoted entirely to you. Day after day after day of talk that will gradually shape—as a stream does the stones that it courses over—our brains, create in them enough little indents and side pockets that we'll be able to retain and form words of our own, if only enough of them to finally ask: what is it that you want, and how can we get it for you?

The side door opened a third time. Just a crack. I saw Huge-Head's hand. It pushed the door open wider. There was a leash, and then, at its end, weakly, Lucy.

He started walking her over to the car. My nose was going fiercely all along the open window top: rust-blood and exhausted flesh, the richly foul aroma of life's full expenditure.

The car door opened.

"It's Angelly, Luce."

Head-tilt.

"Your brother, Angus."

He kind of forced her snout into mine. I licked it. She couldn't bother to snarl.

Huge-Head then leaned over and put his lips on Lucy's head. I've had many of these, his or her lips pressed with such will and want and longing against my head. Is it all right that they don't ever accrue in us? That as deeply as you plant them, they don't ever really take?

He wiped some of that salty water from his eyes. Lucy was led back inside. That was the last I saw of her. Some days later a sealed flowered can that smells vaguely of bone meal was placed on top of the cabin woodstove. Sometimes they go over to it. Pick it up. Call it Lucy.

Head-tilt.

I've been alone here ever since, left to tend this place on my own. As useless as Lucy was for fighting, I could at least count on her idle growls and barks to create a bit of a buffer between me and the threats of the moving world; to put some measure of doubt in the heart of an aggressor. Suddenly it was all on me to patrol the borders of our terrain and plug up any potential holes in my defense of it.

Jock, one-beat tug, my father.

I had a dream about him up in the cabin loft the same night Lucy left us. He's sitting on a horse in the lap of his owner, a man known as an earthstopper. They ride out together at dawn across Devon's stiled seaside pastures. Every so often Jock jumps down, disappears into the mist and finds a foxhole. This is his job. What he was bred to do. The earthstopper dismounts, follows after my father, stops the hole up with his spade. The two of them then get back on their horse and go on riding in search of the next hole, and the next, riding throughout the morning until all the holes they can find are filled, and the fox has nowhere to hide, and the day's hunt can begin.

Their work done, Jock and the earthstopper ride off together, as they always do, to one of the cliffside barrows built by the ancient men in order to get some sleep there above the sea, far away from the frenzy of the hunt: the horns sounding from the distant lodge, the roar of charging horse hooves, the resonant silence in the wake of the slaughter.

But on this day the hunt never happens. Jock and the earthstopper drift off to sleep, hearing no horns, no hooves, no clamor. The earth is eerily silent, as though all of you really had left it, gone away, allowing all the creatures you'd chased to the brink of their own undesired desertion to reemerge again, to come forward to the very borders of your fires and fear boundaries and then cross and reclaim them.

The earthstopper awakes to find that the very foxes he'd left no place to hide have circled in about the edges of his barrow, snarling, poised to attack. Only Jock is holding them off, charging out when they get too close, keeping the lot of them at bay.

I pawed and woofed myself awake that morning, right back into my life's core of sweet-cream and barleybear-musk. I began to work outward from that, ordering all scents here—good and bad, kindly and threatening—around that, charging out each day in all directions from the cabin, through the uncut fields, into the outlying woods, plugging up all the holes, scaring off whatever lurks there.

I became like the spider I sometimes watch in one of the cabin's back windows, my crisscrossed paths through these fields arrayed like his gossamer threads full across the borders of the top corner windowpane, a web woven outward, around himself, and all that he cares for, waiting for the first tremblings of an intruder.

One day it was a deer fly, caught at the web's edge. I watched it, beating itself against the appearance of open sky, climbing, climbing, only to collapse from exhaustion, the spider watching from the opposite corner.

Then it came down, lightly tapped one wing, withdrew, trailing a single thread, a slack sunbeam, all that was needed to reel its prey across a backdrop of hay fronds and swaying treetops, homeward.

How quickly I went from being the spider to becoming the fly.

18

"An—gus!"

At last. He's right there, beside her, the two of them, by the front door, good and angry.

"An—gus, come!"

She's holding a flashlight. They have their boots on, have the same pressing, urgent lean to their bodies that they had the night I treed the porcupine, and they had to come into the woods to get me, come right up to the base of the tree and pull me off it.

He's walking away now, toward the car. He's going to start the engine. Then they'll know. Know something's happened. Have to come farther out.

She's going to be very frightened when she sees me.

But she'll quickly gather herself, get down to the business of helping me. She is more me.

Hold on, Angus.

When you're back, and among them again, and there's no one to blame, and they stop thinking about it, and just let, as I do, their senses take over, they'll see what you've done. They'll look out over these fields and count in the low-wheeling sunlight all the tamped-down shiny threads of your wide web of work here, and know what you've done.

I was so sure of things. Never thought . . . How did this happen?

There was a day some weeks ago. I was down at the pond, scaring the bank scum, putting my paws in the mud to watch the tadpoles squiggle outward like the rays of a doused sun. I sniffed the usual tracks of the different late-night pond sippers: moose, deer, a bobcat. Watched birds dart in and out of the shoreline trees, and dragon-flies dangle above the cattails.

Then I felt it. It came at first as a palpable press upon the day from the far bank, the air above it being filled up by the sure, unhurried movements of a confident predator, and then by its scent: a dank, woolen, rankness.

I ran toward it, my bark going high and frayed, skirting the pond's edge, until reaching only the creature's absence, the residue of its scent. I trailed that awhile into the woods, but sighted nothing.

For nights afterward up in the loft bed, I fell off into the woofs and paw swipes in pursuit of him, the nameless, the primordial me.

Will they remember, what a patient, noiseless creature their "little shit" would become in the days after this first encounter. No more scorch-bark charges into the outer woods at the first little hoof-squeak in the pond mud of a passing deer.

I was choosing my fights now, keeping closer to our rotting quarters, waiting for what would come just today, a big thwack in the outer threads of my web, all at once and purposeful, no attendant struggling, no attempt to flee.

This was "I'm here now. What will you do?" I felt certain it was the same one I'd come upon down by the pond, a loner, I decided, broken off from his pack, looking to forage in my terrain.

They were sitting right over there when it happened, Huge-Head and Sweet-Voice, in the field beside the rose hedge, reading, completely unaware. I went over to her. They'll remember. It will come to them later, how I tried to let her know that this night might be different.

I stayed by them the rest of the afternoon, watched as they cooked their dinner at the stone fire pit, carried it into the cabin, settled in for the night. I was with them there for a time. But the door was open, and I slipped out for my evening foray, the one they've always marked from inside the cabin by the trajectory of my barks through the outlying fields before coming outside around sundown to start calling my name.

He was right back there, had positioned himself a short ways inside the tree line. I ran. Did I hesitate even the slightest bit? Is that what happened?

I went in among the trees, right at him, and I remember now the feel of my fangs first, going deep into his flesh, the popping sound before the warm give.

But I'd gotten only his flank. This gave him a real good shot at my own, the scissor-flash and pop taking just enough of my breath that I released my jaws, and then I was lost, the suddenly free-flying front of me getting a glimpse of just how hopelessly: a mother coyote lying on her side at the base of an old maple, a litter of pups pulling, closed-eyed, at that warm stream of mother milk I used to swim along back in the teat, tummy, and straw of the Combe.

The second bite came hard and fast at my neck, the way I do it when I mean it, and there was a sudden blanching of the night's stars as I hit the ground, a spreading blister of light.

Would you, if I lead you even there, follow me now, frictionless, around that bend.

It was me, or the likes of me, who guided the ancient men even at the end of their days, lying beside them in their barrow rooms for the long sleep in the sea mist and the journey to where the limits lift.

It was me, or the likes of me, they found curled in the arms of men buried twelve thousand years ago in desert tombs.

You and me are everywhere tonight within this wide world's slow-whorling tumuli: our intertwined bones. I can feel them right here in this ground, the long-forgotten burial mounds where dead Indian children were laid to rest with me, or the likes of me, atop their chests, to help lead their souls outward, past their present frames, where they can pour down through The Dipper's bottomless cup into ever new ones.

There!

The car engine!

A little farther, Angus, if only to the wild rose hedge and the outer glow of the cabin light.

Wait! Silence now. Has he gotten out of the car? Where are the peepers? I can't hear them.

Hold on, Angus, to anything, to the earth's revolve, to the last stupid little dead-end memory shards of your days here, things you felt so fervently because you never expected to feel them again.

That mushroom I found one morning along a wood trail in the feathery light of a thousand ferns, nosing it off its stem in order to tunnel farther and farther down into that musty molder, into the folds of its fine-fanned undercup.

The old stone pasture wall on the far side of the entrance road. I was walking along the top of it, following a trail of lichens until the wall crumbled and fell away into a shimmery pool of sunlight being spilled by a stand of aspen.

There is a huge chunk of quartz at the base of an oak in the deep woods by an old deserted bear den. I'd take you to it if I could, a rock whiter than any cloud, with sprigs of moss on it like green ice crystals on the face of tonight's moon.

What good is any of this now? Am I getting any closer? Is this how you convey yourselves?

Fireflies, then. They smell like broken blades of grass. Bumblebees, like over-churned butter. Snakes, like slime.

What is that light? He's turned on the headlights. Keep going, Angus.

Birds are crazy. Noisy, winged sundials. All day long they chirp, as soon as the first tincture of sun hits the dormers above the loft bed. One bird has a rising and falling song that sounds just like little fly-away pieces of Sweet-Voice's cries, calling to me: "Where are you, Angelly Spangelly Spangelly?"

Moths? They really want to be wood. Spend most of their days pressed against it, trying to become it. Moth atoms, I think, are on their way to being wood.

Owls? Theirs is the only birdsong I can sleep to.

Bats. They fly around us all night in the cabin. Huge-Head and Sweet-Voice have no idea. Strange things, bats, but I like them.

I'm so tired. They'll have to do the rest now.

If I'm not here when you come, no longer here for you to hold up in your strange lights, I think I'll still remain in you, the imprint of me, of my simpler, more urgent atoms urging yours farther on.

Once more the car engine.

There. She's right there, her outline in the headlights. She has only to turn left and come a few steps to see me.

"Is anyone coming for him?"

That's what she said that night. I remember it. A bitter winter's night in Cornwall. The three of us are walking along the stone wharf of a tiny seaside village, all cut out of granite. Huge-Head has me snug against him in his coat. Lights, strung in the shapes of dragons and spangelly indoor pine trees, bob and sway in the harbor.

Head-tilt.

They are talking to each other. Talking of something called the mousehole cat, some lucky cat who gets to live in a mousehole. Up ahead of us people are gathered along the wharf railing, leaning over it, staring down to where the slope of the stone boat ramp meets the slapping sea.

We go closer. It looks like a shiny black bag of sand. Then it moves, the harbor lights suddenly bleeding across the twisting back of a stranded sea lion with a broken forelimb. It tries to fin its way up into the village, falters, rears back again, barks.

Everyone points and watches. Some are standing alone, shuffling their feet, smoking, occasionally staring out across the sea. Others are embracing, pulling each other close, staring into each other.

"Isn't anyone coming for him?" Sweet-Voice says. "Someone must be coming."

I still see him—ancient, sea-bound me—his tiny

fur-tipped ears, the long-whiskered snout drawing back, slowly opening in a wide, starward gape.

"Oh, Angus!"

That's her, hurrying toward me now, her outline all funny in the glare, like she's getting tangled in it, waving her arms for him to come, too, saying my name, over and over, calling to me ever more softly as she nears.

"Oh, Angus, I'm sorry."

She doesn't want to touch me. Doesn't even know where to begin to touch me.

Later, when I'm back among them, they'll remember how I went up to her earlier this afternoon here in the north field, how she had to pull me away from her. That was a first.

I hopped up onto her lap, knocked off her book, went right into those needy hands, and then farther and on. I put my head on her shoulder. Every atom said to. I even left it there for a while.

She grabbed me with both hands, held me away from her, my front legs sticking straight out. She shook me, pulled my paws up beside my ears, smooshed them against my head.

"Mister . . ." she said, biting her bottom lip that way she does when she's speaking her sweet nonsense to me.

"Mister . . . I met a man."

epilogue

Cabin Journal
August 8, 1999

ANGUS IS DEAD.

We found him a week ago tonight in the north field between the base of the crab apple tree and the island hedgerow of wild roses. I don't know how far he had to crawl to get to us, but he did, and was still alive when we found him.

He'd fought so hard, and once we'd gotten him to the vet, and then to the surgeon, I was sure he was going to live. But so much time was lost that night and his injuries were too severe.

Bex and I had been calling to him, on and off, for well over an hour. That has pretty much been the routine with him since we got here this spring. Angus has always done just what he wanted. From our first days with him in Cornwall, he refused to walk on the leash, always had to lead, darting out ahead of us along the ocean-cliff paths, a five-pound sprite going right up to the very edge of a 300-foot precipice, before briefly reporting back as though to say, "Okay. I've checked everything out, you can come along now."

The first few weeks here he had us throwing on the billy boots every night and heading out with the flashlight only to find him bouncing about the base of a tree he'd scared something up, or worrying the entrance to some other creature's burrow. We'd stand there calling to him, and he'd completely ignore us. When Angus got his heart set on something, you had to walk over and pull him off of it. It would take Lucy five or six summers up here to meet with her first porcupine. Angus came back to the cabin with a face full of quills on his second day.

I keep going over the events of that night now, wondering if we were too careless, wondering if it wasn't Angus's own carelessness that made for ours with him here. It kills me to think of the two of us sitting in that cabin, watching a movie—I can't even remember what it was—while he was trying to make his way back. I kept telling Bex not to worry, that we'd been through all this before, that any minute he'd be at the door, issuing the clipped, one-beat bark that meant he wanted to be let in.

It was well past nine when we finally decided to start the car. A clear night, lots of stars, a three-quarter moon coming up above the mountain opposite ours, but not far enough yet into the low arc that it makes this time of year across the southern horizon to light the surrounding fields. Bex stood by the front door with a flashlight. I revved the engine, again and again. Nothing. Then I turned on the headlights.

Bex said it was when she turned to avert her eyes from the glare that she saw in the distance a fleck of white which she at first took to be the tufted rug we'd bought months ago back in Penzance to cushion Angus's travel crate for the flight back to the States. We'd thrown the crate out when we got back to Brooklyn last January, Angus having rendered it useless with all his assaults on the door latches. But we saved the rug for him to use as a car pillow, and the day after we arrived, he promptly dragged it out into the north field and began maniacally tearing and growling at the thing as though he bore it some deep, lasting grudge.

I watched Bex walking toward the north field, and then I saw her running, out of her mind, screaming and waving back at me. I got out, ran up to her, stooped over in the grass above Angus. His face. I can still see it. It wasn't him—his eyes fixed, unseeing, his jaws clenched tight, teeth bared, air faintly puffing out sideways as though he was still latched on to whatever had gotten him.

We didn't know whether to touch him, where to touch him. His coat was wet, matted with saliva and dirt, but there was hardly any blood. Bex yelled at me to go get work gloves from the cabin, thinking that Angus might try to bite, but he was in deep shock. I lifted him onto Lucy's old bed. His neck had swollen to twice its normal size, and there were trapped air pockets all under his coat. It buckled and popped to the touch like tin foil.

It was a Sunday night. We didn't know any vets here in Quebec, so we decided to rush him to the one where we'd had Lucy put down, about twenty minutes over the border in Vermont.

We'd spend the whole night with him there, taking turns holding an oxygen mask over his face, while the vet—a young woman, just out of school, this was her first emergency case—got him on intravenous fluids.

Over the course of the night, we managed to bring Angus out of shock and his body temperature—perilously low when we arrived—back to normal. Soon he was responding to his name, weakly wagging his tail when we called to him or when he saw one of us coming back into the room. The vet had even begun talking to us about taking him home.

I remember sitting there with him for the next half hour or so, Bex and I taking turns holding the oxygen mask over his nose, talking to him, fantasizing about getting him back here and nursing him, day by day, back to health. And for the longest time, it seemed time had stopped, that we were all adrift in our own fatigue and the absence of thought, buoyed up only by the apparent recovery and rising spirits of Angus there before us on the table, tail still wagging.

Then something changed. I'm still not sure what happened, but the vet started telling us that she was concerned about how labored Angus's breathing still was, that it wasn't stabilizing, and that maybe it was time we thought about making a decision. In the matter of a half hour we'd somehow gone from taking him home to putting him down. It was as though we'd fallen asleep on our feet and were suddenly being awakened hours later by an entirely different person.

I lost it. Said I wasn't going to lose two dogs in a month. Said I wanted everything possible done, and wanted to know why we hadn't even taken X rays yet to find out what we later would about the full extent of Angus's internal injuries: the punctured chest cavity that had already collapsed one lung and was putting a considerable amount of pressure on the other, the lacerated liver, the ruptured kidneys and ureter.

She said, nervously, something about not being able to turn on the X-ray machine until the place opened for regular office hours and then excused herself to make a phone call. When she got back, the conversation would shift to the possibility of emergency surgery. We were told that there was a specialist in Burlington who might be able to assemble a team and fly up to us.

They go very slowly, moments of urgency. So many thoughts and questions run through your head in so little time, it's as though you're living a little condensed life within each tick of the clock: Yes, get the surgeon here right away, and how the hell are we going to pay for this, and why didn't we make this decision a few hours ago, and might we have if a more experienced vet were on hand, and how would we be behaving if this were our child here before us.

It was an eerie, emotional limbo that we'd entered. We spoke of it even at the time. For all the comments one hears about a dog being just like one of the family, the situation we found ourselves in that night exposed subtle gradations in the depth of the emotional attachments we form. As hard as we were fighting for Angus, we found ourselves fighting as well this deep inner tug toward resignation and surrender. There was both a dim recognition of, and a sense of self-rebuke over, the fact that we weren't doing more, weren't rushing him to surgery in an ambulance, or even a helicopter, or weren't strangling that young vet and demanding a more experienced one.

And even if we had unlimited resources, and could have indulged every emotion, every option with Angus—the vet told us at one point that the best thing for him would be to get him to a special veterinary hospital in Rochester, New York—the fact is that there isn't the ready infrastructure in place for dog emergencies that there is for our own, and that alone bespeaks an obvious and perhaps natural and healthy, I don't know, sense of hierarchy in our conception of ourselves and other creatures.

A call finally came from the surgeon in Burlington. He was unable to get a team together. Could we possibly get

Angus to him, about a two-hour drive south? It was about eight in the morning by then. The office was just opening up for regular work hours. The vet advised that we go back to the cabin and get a few hours' sleep, by which time she'd have worked out the travel equipment and gotten a complete set of X rays for us to take down with us to the surgeon.

It was close to noon by the time we got back to the vet's office. Angus was lying inside an empty glass aquarium, with a plastic lid over the top, a tube stuck through one corner leading from a tank of oxygen. We transported the whole rig to the backseat of the car and sped off, me driving, Bex in back, watching over Angus.

The directions we'd been given were totally wrong, far too indirect, but Bex had the map out and managed to devise an alternate route that wound up saving us at least an hour. The big worry was the oxygen. Bex had been keeping an eye on the gauge the entire trip, watching it dip lower and lower, and then about thirty miles north of our destination we ran out.

She started screaming. At first she thought it best to leave the lid on the tank and let Angus breathe the last of the oxygen inside, but it was so hot that day that the tank was steaming up, so Bex just tore the lid off and threw open all the car windows, trying to get Angus as much fresh air as possible.

He managed, somehow, to hold on. We pulled into the surgeon's lot. There was already an assistant waiting for us. She ran up to the car, took one end of the aquarium, and with me holding the other, we rushed Angus inside. The doctor stepped out of the room to review the X rays and upon returning promptly told us to get the hell out of there, to go home. He said the last thing he wanted for Angus, should he pull through the surgery, was to have him get all worked up over the sight of us.

It was early evening by the time we got back. I was sitting out here by the fire pit, just staring off, exhausted. Bex was trying to busy herself about the cabin, preparing dinner. We hadn't been back an hour when the phone call came. Angus had apparently survived two cardiac arrests before succumbing to a third. They were never able to stabilize his breathing in order to get to the extensive and very delicate surgery that would have been required.

"Your little dog was some fighter," the doctor said.

I started asking the inevitable pointless questions: whether it would have made a difference if we'd gotten Angus into surgery sooner, if there hadn't been so much time wasted. The surgeon said we'd done all we could, had done more than a lot of people would have.

And that was it. Angus gone at only eleven months.

It's gotten awfully still around here now. We were just saying earlier today that we might have packed up already and gone back to Brooklyn if it weren't for our subletter. Odd to suddenly feel the need to get some distance from the very place we've come to each year to get away from everything.

It's like we're living in a damn dog mausoleum, two cans of ashes now up on the woodstove, and all around the land, reminders of them: Lucy's cupped indent still there in the grass beneath the fireside silver birch, and, just about everywhere I look, Angus's mad desire lines through the tall field grass, and his mauled sticks, and the strewn, withering carcasses of his many conquests—mice, moles, toads, frogs, snakes.

Just now another white-throated sparrow—its song so distinctive that, paradoxically, you can read whatever you want into it—seemed to be calling out from the silver birch here beside me: "Where are you, Angelly, Spangelly, Spangelly?"—a question one of them almost got the definitive answer to a few weeks ago, flying off just ahead of Angus's ever-busy bite.

I still can't believe he isn't here. That's just how here

he was. When we had to put Lucy down, I remember being shocked by how fast she slipped away. Bex and I both held her in our arms as the injection was given and within seconds she was gone. It takes so much energy for something to live, it seemed impossible, wrong to me, that it would all dissipate that quickly, like a blown-out candle. But with Angus it feels as though that much energy has to continue somewhere. I often find myself looking over my shoulder, fully expecting to see his proud little tough-guy prance coming toward me here through the field.

Bex told me just today that Angus actually spoke to her shortly after we'd left him for the last time. It was on the car ride back from the surgeon's. We were nearly home, coming up one of the last turns in the mountain road that leads to our entrance. It was one very loud, clear bark, she said, the one he sounds when he wants, finally, to be let in.

The wind has picked up again, that horrible, hollow sound of it washing over the treetops. Whenever I look out over these long familiar woods now, I feel a sense of anger and edginess. I've thought more than once about buying a gun, but Bex is against it.

We've had, and have heard, all kinds of ideas about what Angus tangled with that night. The farmer down the road here says it might have been a fox, but given Angus's breeding, I think he could have held his own with a fox.

A bear. A bobcat. There are some of those around here still. I found bobcat tracks in the pond mud last summer and bear droppings in the woods early one spring. But Angus bore hardly any signs of the kind of claw marks one would expect from an encounter with either of those.

It's funny how everyone, every man, I should say, to whom we've told the story of Angus's death—whether it's someone from around here or a friend back in the city—every one of them has come up with his own theory about what happened, stating it with that preemptive certainty that we men always adopt when discussing such matters.

"Wolf. Yep. Sounds like a wolf to me."

"Coyotes. Definitely coyotes, but I'm surprised they didn't drag him off."

We've heard wolverine, a fisher, even a wolf-dog hybrid. I remember at the vet with Angus that night, staring at a sign on the wall behind the examining table: "All wolf-hybrids must be muzzled before receiving treatment."

A local handyman who came up here a couple of weeks ago to help me fix some loose sections of the cabin's tin roof owns a ninety-percent wolf. He says they instantly bond with immediate family members, but that's as far as their loyalties and affections go. He told us about a friend of his who'd come up the front walk of his place one day last winter to pay a visit. He usually kept the animal on a chain in back, but it happened to be in the house this day. The friend unwittingly opened the front door and wound up in the hospital with seventy stitches in the forearm he used to keep his throat from getting ripped open.

We see ads for wolf-hybrids all the time here in the local papers and in *Uncle Henry's Swap or Sell It Guide*. I bought one a few days after Angus died. I like to thumb through it by the fire at night. It's somehow consoling now to read about dogs I have no intention of buying. "88% wolf pups," went one of the ads, "Father Classic Gray Wolf, mother Black Timberwolf. Will sell only to wolf lovers with good homes." That last phrase, I don't know, it sort of sums up for me the inherent awkwardness of our relationship with the wild.

I suppose it makes no difference, finally, what it was that got Angus, but after what happened here last night, we now think we have a pretty good idea. Bex and I had driven into town to have dinner and get away from this place for a few hours at least. We arrived back at about ten o'clock, around the same time we found Angus a week ago. Bex went straight into the cabin, but I decided to head out into the north field here to take in some of the cool night air and the stars.

I was standing just behind the rose hedgerow when the howling started. It was coming from very close, just down there inside the tree line, directly beneath the bottom corner star of the Big Dipper. It went on for minutes, a timeless, stirring sound that instantly claims you and the night and whatever prey has been felled within it.

At one point, amidst the yips and howls and very dog-like woofs, I heard what sounded more like the yelping of young pups, and right then a picture coalesced in my mind of what probably happened that night, the edges of Angus's territory suddenly claimed by a coyote pack with a pregnant or newly nursing mother, and Angus, being who he was, charging out to confront them. I can't say for sure why they didn't "drag him off," but they were probably more concerned with protecting the mother and the pups.

It all seems so clear-cut. That, curiously, is the only real solace we take now from what's happened, the inevitability of it, the pure remorselessness of the wild and of Angus's fearful charge into it, into something at once of him and much greater than him, the jaws of his own ancestry, the part that never came along with us.

It's getting late, the sun's dropping toward the pine tree tops. Time to get the fire started. Time to get on with it. Bex is still out there somewhere walking in the woods. I should call her. She misses Angus terribly, has said from the beginning that she felt this incredible bond with him, that he was more her dog.

He knew, I think, all along, what was going to happen. He even tried to let Bex know, did something he never had before, hopping up into Bex's lap as we sat over in the north field reading that afternoon, and then laying his head across her shoulder.

It's a bit scary how attached we get to dogs. There's something deep within our respective beings that connects us to them. I was reading not long ago about the Huron Indians, who used to roam these very woods, how they, along with countless other cultures, thought of dogs as our ongoing link with our own purer, simpler selves in the wholeness of nature; as our eyes into both the primal world and the world beyond this one. They'd often bury their dead children with a dog curled up on each child's chest so that its soul would be guided to the next life along the Milky Way, or what the Huron called "the path of souls." Dogs are said to go along with us there as well, following an adjacent stretch of stars known as "the path of dogs."

I don't know where that much energy goes. I don't really think in terms of places like heaven or a hereafter so much as I do a state of eased, of disassembled atoms, everywhere the free-flying matter of existence awaiting new shapes, new assignments. It's something like words before they're set down on a page. It's the blankness of the page, inspiration without expression, pure urge, if we can imagine, if we can even stand that.

Even now, when I find myself getting carried away with all the second-guessing, and the recriminations for letting Angus be out so late that night, and for not going out sooner and farther into the darkness to look for him; if I just start missing him too much, I have only to invoke his spirit to get ahold of myself, the echo energy of his no-look-back, full-throttle approach to life, urging me to get over the loss of his.

He was different, that dog, restless in his own atoms, forever charging around the next bend. He's arrived there now, but I feel he's part of us still, is all around us still. We see him here at night whenever we look up at the Dipper and the darkness flowing through its bottomless cup, or by day, staring out over these fields, the late-slanting sunlight turning the multi-spoked wheel of his furiously brief charge across this earth.

about the author

CHARLES SIEBERT WAS BORN IN BROOKLYN, NEW York, where he currently resides. He is the author of the memoir *Wickerby: An Urban Pastoral.* His poems, essays, and articles have appeared in numerous publications, including *The New Yorker, The New York Times Magazine, Harper's Magazine, Outside,* and *Esquire.*